Networking Mastery Unleashed

Elevate Your Pro Skills

Copyrights 2024

All rights reserved

Table of Contents

INTRODUCTION 5

CHAPTER 1: THE ADVANCED NETWORKING MINDSET 7

STRATEGIES FOR CULTIVATING A NETWORKING MINDSET 8
ELEVATING EMPATHY: THE FOUNDATION OF ADVANCED CONNECTION................10
STRATEGIC NETWORKING: APPROACHING HIGH-STAKES SITUATIONS WITH CONFIDENCE 12
SUMMARY 15

CHAPTER 2: MASTERING INFLUENCE AND PERSUASION......................17

ACTIVE LISTENING ON A DEEPER LEVEL: MINING FOR GOLDEN NUGGETS 19
BUILDING RAPPORT: THE ART OF INSTANT AND DEEP CONNECTION......................21
ADVANCED PERSUASION TECHNIQUES: FORGING MUTUALLY BENEFICIAL COLLABORATIONS 23
SUMMARY 25

CHAPTER 3: STRATEGIC ONLINE NETWORKING IN THE VIRTUAL FRONTIER 27

BEYOND BASICS: UNLEASHING LINKEDIN'S FULL NETWORKING POTENTIAL...........30
CRAFTING A CAPTIVATING DIGITAL BRAND: YOUR ONLINE NETWORKING MAGNET.32
VIRTUAL POWER NETWORKING: ADVANCED TACTICS FOR ONLINE ENGAGEMENT ...34
SUMMARY 36

CHAPTER 4: COMMANDING ATTENTION: PUBLIC SPEAKING AND STORYTELLING 37

OWNING THE STAGE: ADVANCED PUBLIC SPEAKING FOR NETWORKING EVENTS 39
MASTERFUL STORYTELLING: MAKING YOUR EXPERIENCES MEMORABLE 41
CAPTIVATING COMMUNICATION: TECHNIQUES FOR UNFORGETTABLE NETWORKING 43

SUMMARY 46

CHAPTER 5: STRATEGIC RELATIONSHIP BUILDING 48

NETWORKING WITH INTENTION: MAPPING YOUR CONNECTIONS 50
NAVIGATING COMPLEX NETWORKS: STRATEGIES FOR MULTI-DIMENSIONAL CONNECTION 52
DEEPENING CONNECTIONS: STRATEGIES FOR LONG-TERM, MUTUALLY BENEFICIAL RELATIONSHIPS 54
SUMMARY 56

CHAPTER 6: HIGH-LEVEL ENGAGEMENT AND EXECUTIVE NETWORKING 58

NETWORKING WITH INDUSTRY TITANS: APPROACHING LEADERS WITH CONFIDENCE 61
ESTABLISHING C-SUITE CONNECTIONS: ADVANCED TECHNIQUES FOR HIGH-LEVEL NETWORKING 62
LEARNING FROM THE BEST: GAINING MENTORSHIP FROM INDUSTRY PIONEERS 65
SUMMARY 68

CHAPTER 7: NETWORKING ACROSS CULTURES AND BORDERS 70

CULTURAL INTELLIGENCE IN NETWORKING: EXCELLING IN GLOBAL CONNECTIONS ...71
BUILDING INTERNATIONAL NETWORKS: ADVANCED CROSS-BORDER STRATEGIES....73
SUMMARY 76

CHAPTER 8: TAKING ADVANTAGE OF INTERNATIONAL OPPORTUNITIES 78

THRIVING IN GLOBAL CONFERENCES AND SEMINARS...80
STRATEGIC INTERNATIONAL COLLABORATIONS: FORGING PARTNERSHIPS WITH IMPACT 82
INTERNATIONAL JOB HUNTING: ADVANCED NETWORKING FOR GLOBAL OPPORTUNITIES..84
SUMMARY 86

CHAPTER 9: CRISIS MANAGEMENT AND NETWORKING RESILIENCE 88

Networking during Crisis: Navigating Adversities with Skill 90
Rebuilding After Reputational Challenges: Advanced Networking Damage Control 92
Networking Resilience: Emerging Stronger from Challenges 94
Summary 95

CHAPTER 10: NETWORKING FOR PERSONAL GROWTH AND IMPACT 97

Networking for Social Change: Influencing Causes You Believe In 99
Personal Development through Networking: Strategies for Lifelong Growth 101
Building a Legacy: Transforming Networking into Lasting Contributions 102
Summary 103

CONCLUSION 105

Introduction

Hello and welcome to the networking mastery. Either you have read my initial book, Network Like a Pro - The Ultimate Guide to Networking, OR you already consider yourself a Networking Expert and are ready to take your networking to the next level. Either way - let's go! Now, be ready to explore the depths of "Networking Mastery Unleashed" and go on a life-changing adventure. I am about to reveal a wealth of advanced techniques, insider knowledge, and realistic simulations in this all-encompassing book, all of which have been painstakingly designed to push your networking abilities to previously unheard-of levels. As I provide you with the skills and information necessary to confidently and deftly negotiate the complex web of professional connections, be ready to rise above the ordinary and embrace the remarkable.

This is a guide to unleashing the full power of your networking expertise, not simply another networking handbook. The days of passing acquaintances and brief exchanges are long gone. Through "Networking Mastery Unleashed," you will delve into the art and science of creating significant, cross-cultural relationships that have a lasting effect. This book is meant to meet you where you are in your professional relationship-building journey and help you go to the next level, whether you are an experienced networker or just getting started.

By reading my book, you will get to know advanced methods beyond the fundamentals and uncover opportunities and secret reservoirs of influence that are not readily apparent when using conventional networking techniques. Each chapter is expertly chosen to provide you with the knowledge and strategies required to succeed in any professional context, from developing active listening skills to handling high-stakes scenarios with poise.

"Networking Mastery Unleashed" emphasizes implementation above just imparting information. You can put theory into practice and refine your abilities in real-world situations by engaging in real-life simulations and practical activities. With the skills and tactics required to win, you'll be ready to take on any situation—networking events, high-stakes negotiations, or online connection building.

So be ready for a learning, development, and change-filled voyage. As you delve into "Networking Mastery Unleashed," be ready to push yourself, broaden your perspective, and seize previously unattainable chances. By the time you turn the last page, you'll be more than simply an expert networker—you'll be a relationship- and industry-building influencer, prepared to make a lasting impression. Remember, you never know where a conversation will take you - Go Forth and Network Like a Master!

To Your Massive Success!

Emmelie Forsyth

Author and Founder of Network Like a Pro

www.networklikeapro.com

Chapter 1: The Advanced Networking Mindset

This chapter explores the skill of making deeper connections with people. The goal is to cultivate a mindset that promotes deep connections. "Strategies for Cultivating a Networking Mindset," will teach you how to handle the challenges involved in professional networking. The "Strategic Networking" portion provides insights into effectively managing high-stakes situations, while the "Elevating Empathy" section emphasizes the significance of understanding people. The foundation for mastering advanced networking abilities is laid forth in this chapter.

Developing your network is a lifelong talent, and it is not only something you must do when applying for jobs. Building and updating your network throughout your career is essential. The best time to do this is before you need it.

These are the three golden guidelines that networking experts consistently follow.

Be a giver. You attract other individuals to you if you develop an attitude of kindness. What valuable possessions do you have that others could find interesting? Like everyone else, you have some connections. You are knowledgeable and equipped with information. You're gifted in a few areas. You have some time and energy left over, at least. These are all the networking equivalent of money.

As a provider, you strive to always provide something in return for requests that are made. If you cannot answer, you offer to assist the information seeker in expanding or exploring their possibilities. Being a provider means staying conscious of the issues and causes important to you, making it easier to spot opportunities when they present themselves. You understand that being a provider is typically beneficial for you and the person or organization asking, so you don't reflexively say "no" to save time. When givers see that you are a giver, they become even more giving.

Be a joiner. Joining professional groups is the evident low-hanging fruit, but don't stop there—don't limit yourself to monthly meetings after you become a member. Choose a club activity, priority, or mission piques your interest, then volunteer for a committee or unique project. The best part is that you develop new friendships that will benefit you in the future, you enhance your professional reputation and profile by keeping your word, and you may even enjoy yourself and feel like you've accomplished something. An accomplished networker can reach further into their community and find something they are interested in participating in, be it business, the arts, special needs, education, or any other endeavor that brings people together.

Be a caretaker. Building relationships by donating and joining requires nurturing, much like investing in other long-term partnerships. Caring people stay in touch. Their interests are in being useful and up-to-date. Everybody wants to be seen, heard, and appreciated, and the most significant network connections are formed through similar interests and time investment, much like your closest friends.

The most apparent blind spot in networking is the job seeker's desperate attempts to "build my network." That isn't how it functions. You must have been building your network all along if you want it to be there for you when needed. It is a garden that requires care.

Strategies for Cultivating a Networking Mindset

In today's highly interconnected world, building a solid network is a crucial skill that can lead to countless opportunities. Learning the skill of networking is essential, whether your goals are to grow your social circle, establish business ties, or progress your career. But how precisely does one cultivate a networking mindset if networking doesn't come easily to them?

Intakes help you succeed in the realm of professional connections. This piece examines a few essential techniques and concepts.

The Power of Networking in the Digital Age

It is simple to underestimate the enduring significance of human connection in a time when technology and automation rule the roost. Even though digital communication and internet platforms are widely available, research shows that over 88% of professionals believe networking is essential to their career advancement. This emphasizes how important it is to build and maintain relationships in today's extremely competitive environment.

Key Strategies for Cultivating a Networking Mindset

- **Be Proactive:** Don't wait for opportunities to come to you—actively seek out networking events, conferences, and industry gatherings where you may meet like-minded individuals. The first step to developing a strong network is to take the initiative to put oneself out there, whether that means joining online networking groups or going to local meetups.

- **Foster Genuine Connections:** Building connections on LinkedIn and gathering business cards aren't the only aspects of networking. It's about creating deep connections based on respect for one another and shared interests. Spend some time getting to know people personally, paying close attention to what they have to say, and looking for areas of agreement that you can build on to deepen your relationship.

- **Give Prior to Receiving:** When networking, adopt a generous and reciprocal perspective. Don't ask for anything in return; instead, provide your connections with resources, counsel, and support. Being someone else's valued resource will automatically attract opportunities and goodwill.

- **Utilize Internet Platforms:** Don't undervalue the importance of Internet networking, even while in-person contacts are priceless. You can join groups relevant to your sector, network with professionals, and demonstrate your expertise through content sharing and participation on platforms like LinkedIn. Here are our best suggestions for networking at virtual events if you're giving a virtual speech soon.

- **Follow Up and Stay Engaged:** After establishing a new relationship, maintain it. Thank you for the conversation, and propose some methods to remain in touch with a handwritten note. Staying involved is essential to building and maintaining your network over time, whether setting up a coffee date or making connections on social media.

Embrace the Networking Mindset

Developing a networking mindset involves more than just growing your network; it also entails forming sincere connections, lending a helping hand to others, and grasping chances for advancement and cooperation. By using these essential tactics and ideas, you can fully realize the benefits of networking and set yourself up for success in your personal and professional efforts. Thus, push yourself beyond your comfort zone, believe in the power of connections, and observe as your network grows and opens doors to countless opportunities.

Elevating Empathy: The Foundation of Advanced Connection

Empathy is the foundation of meaningful interactions in advanced networking. In contrast to traditional networking strategies, which often prioritize transactional interactions and self-promotion, advanced networking focuses on comprehending and empathizing with people. Genuine and lasting relationships are based on empathy, which is the capacity to understand and relate to the feelings and experiences of others.

Empathy is actively striving to comprehend the viewpoints, needs, and goals of others with whom one comes into contact. It is not only listening. Proficient networkers understand that empathy is a strategic tool for developing rapport and trust, not just a soft ability. They provide an atmosphere where people feel heard, respected, and appreciated by empathizing with others, which paves the way for genuine relationships to grow.

Among the most essential components of empathy is active listening. Expert networkers know how important it is to focus entirely on others while interacting with them. Instead of trying to control or interrupt other people's interactions, they concentrate on really comprehending the ideas and emotions that their opponents are expressing. They show people they respect and care for them by listening to them and letting them know their opinions are valued.

Furthermore, empathy encompasses a deeper comprehension of the feelings and intentions underpinning human conduct and interactions at a surface level. Understanding that empathy produces compassion and solidarity, advanced networkers make it a point to sympathize with the struggles and goals of their colleagues. By recognizing and approving others' experiences, they foster a feeling of unity and acceptance that surpasses barriers in the workplace.

Empathy is not only comprehending the viewpoints of others but also actively assisting and empowering them. Beyond simple empathy, advanced networkers show compassion in their behaviors. By giving support, resources, or just a listening ear, they aim to lessen the difficulties and responsibilities that their connections must bear. They create links of trust and reciprocity by lending a helpful hand, and these bonds serve as the cornerstone of long-lasting partnerships.

Empathy is essential to negotiating and dispute resolution. Expert networkers realize that miscommunications and arguments will always arise in any connection. Rather than using force or confrontation, they handle disagreements with compassion and an open mind. They look for win-win solutions that preserve relationships and promote respect for one another by trying to comprehend all parties' underlying worries and motives.

Elevating empathy in networking ultimately involves realizing the intrinsic humanity in every engagement and embracing the potential of connection rather than merely being pleasant or agreeable. Expert networkers are aware that empathy is a skill that helps them build longer-lasting, more meaningful connections rather than a sign of weakness. Through the practice of empathy in their networking initiatives, they generate a positive and benevolent ripple effect that surpasses borders and changes lives.

As a result, empathy is the cornerstone of advanced networking, allowing people to create genuine relationships based on respect, trust, and understanding. Advanced networkers provide an atmosphere where meaningful connections may flourish by carefully listening, comprehending the viewpoints of others, acting with compassion, and handling disagreements with empathy.

Strategic Networking: Approaching High-Stakes Situations with Confidence

In the fast-paced world of professional networking, connections are crucial. Project managers may gain from networking, much like lawyers in "Suits," who play high-stakes power games. This essay examines professional networking from a project manager's viewpoint, using influence from "Suits."

Project managers need networking to expand their chances. Reasons why networking is essential:

- **Access to Resources:** A robust network gives resources, knowledge, and assistance to help you solve project challenges.
- **Career Advancement:** Networking may lead to job offers, promotions, and other professional advancements. You'll learn about vacancies before they're publicized and what companies want.
- **Learning and Growth:** Talking to specialists from other fields helps you improve personally and professionally.
- **Problem Solving:** Networking may provide creative solutions and ideas. You can use your network's expertise to solve project problems.
- **Reputation Building:** A strong network boosts your professional reputation. Your coworkers can attest to your expertise.

How to Network Effectively

Learning and perfecting networking takes time. Steps to network effectively:

- **Set Clear Goals:** Whether you want to get a job, learn more, or network with industry leaders, set clear goals.
- **Attend Industry Events:** Participate in conferences, seminars, and workshops related to your field. These events are great for networking.
- **Social Media:** Connect with industry leaders on LinkedIn. Share useful stuff and participate in debates to get attention.

- **Nurture Relationships:** Networking takes time. Stay connected, support others, and care about their success.
- **Give before Getting:** Be helpful to your network. Build enduring relationships by offering value and assistance.

The Four-Suits Methodology Mark Lee

Everybody wore suits back then, the guys at least. Even though suits are less frequent these days, the four suits in a deck of cards may nevertheless serve as a helpful framework for arranging interactions while networking:

Spades: To start, you probe (with your spade, figuratively speaking), breaking the ice and asking general inquiries to learn more about the other person. This entails asking thoughtful, open-ended inquiries without being confrontational;

Hearts: You want to establish a rapport. Finding something with which you have a strong emotional (heartfelt) connection can make this task easier. Are your likes and dislikes comparable to each other's? I still sometimes need to express interest in what the other person has brought up. I so wind up narrowing the discussion on that subject and making it harder to get to the next phase.

Clubs: When the other person enquires about you and your company, introduce yourself less. Try talking about one or two of your customers instead. Being well-prepared and poised to discuss one or more customers who, in some way, belong to the same "club" as the person you are with or the people they know is essential. Your client(s) commended you on your abilities that pertain to anything the other person expressed. They shared equivalent concerns and had similar troubles or problems. Only if you are prepared with various anecdotes about your customers and have done your homework by asking probing questions that will allow you to learn enough about the other person will you be able to pull this off.

Finally, **we have Diamonds**, the most precious suit in our deck. This suit represents the follow-up, a crucial part of networking that is often overlooked. Before you part ways, consider how you can continue the conversation or provide value to the other person. This thoughtful follow-up, be it a shared resource or a piece of advice, can leave a lasting impression.

Following through on your commitments is a key step in establishing your credibility early on. Trust is a vital personal attribute to demonstrate when building business relationships. It's not just about what you say, but about what you do that will earn you the trust of your peers and clients.

Using the "Four Suits" method to have more effective business conversations will help you stand out and increase the likelihood that people will remember, refer, and recommend you—not just in general, but mainly for the kinds of work you enjoy, the types of clients you like, and the pay you deserve.

Summary

To succeed at networking, one needs to have a sophisticated attitude that extends beyond making acquaintances and exchanging business cards. With a strategic focus on establishing deep and enduring connections, this attitude calls for action. It entails developing oneself personally, improving communication, and taking the initiative to form relationships. Finding opportunities for connection and interacting with people in a way that promotes understanding and mutual benefit are critical components of cultivating this mindset.

Empathy is a vital component of the advanced networking attitude. Deeper connections are based on empathy, which enables people to truly comprehend and relate to the needs and feelings of others. Networkers can foster an environment of openness and trust by increasing empathy. This entails being genuinely interested in other people's experiences, listening intently, and displaying compassion.

Stronger and longer-lasting relationships result from more meaningful encounters when empathy is at their core.

Strategic networking entails entering high-stakes scenarios with confidence and a well-thought-out plan. It's essential to meet the appropriate people in the proper situations, not just old individuals. This approach entails preparing beforehand, establishing objectives for every networking opportunity, and using every contact to reach those objectives. Being confident is essential because it enables people to interact with people who can support them in achieving their goals and moving outside their comfort zones. Networkers can enhance the impact of their connections and develop a strong professional network by fusing strategic thinking with empathy.

"When you consider the importance of Word-of-Mouth, referrals, recommendations, and knowledge-sharing do you even have a choice? Your network is your everything." – Vedran Rasic

Chapter 2: Mastering Influence and Persuasion

Establishing rapport and managing persuasion tactic without being seen as manipulative are very intricate areas. In this chapter we will explores the profound potential of active listening, where even the most inconsequential revelations may unveil invaluable prospects. By mastering the methods that generate immediate and significant connections, you can acquire the skills necessary to establish rapport. In summary, investigate sophisticated approaches to persuasion that result in symbiotic collaborations, thereby establishing a strong groundwork for enduring partnerships.

Anyone who wants to speak well and succeed needs persuasion and influence. In a presentation, meeting, or negotiation, you must grab your audience's attention, develop trust and rapport, and inspire action. This will teach you sophisticated audience persuasion strategies.

1. Use the power of storytelling

Stories are an excellent approach to persuade and influence. Stories make your message more memorable and relevant by engaging listeners' emotions, imagination, and memory. Stories also build trust, empathy, and common ground with your audience since they can connect to your experiences. To utilize storytelling successfully, you need an engaging tale with a clear framework, meaningful message, and emotional appeal. Customize your tale to your audience's needs, interests, and beliefs to make an effect and utilize vivid language, gestures, and voice.

2. Apply the principle of reciprocity

Use reciprocity to convince and influence your audience. People feel obligated to repay a favor or a show of generosity. You may employ this technique to generate rapport, make a good impression, and improve audience approval. Give your audience a free sample, discount, praise, or useful suggestion before requesting a purchase, sign-up, or referral. You can also use reciprocity to overcome objections or resistance by acknowledging your audience's concerns, offering concessions, or finding common ground.

3. Leverage the power of social proof

A third way to convince and influence your audience is to use social proof, which is the inclination to follow others' conduct or ideas, particularly when unclear. Social evidence boosts credibility, authority, and trustworthiness, reducing audience doubts and anxieties. You may use testimonials, reviews, ratings, endorsements, or case studies to demonstrate how your product, service, or concept has helped others. You may also support your statements using data, facts, figures, or expert comments. Social proof may also generate urgency or scarcity by indicating how many people have acted or how limited your offer is.

4. Use the power of framing

A fourth strategy to convince and influence your audience is to frame your message to emphasize the benefits, advantages, or opportunities rather than the costs, dangers, or downsides. Frame your message to appeal to your audience's emotions, values, and ambitions and affect their perception and decision-making. Positive framing may highlight the benefits of taking action, such as saving money, time, or health. Negative framing may also highlight the costs of inaction, such as time, money, and health.

5. Use the power of questions

Use questions to engage, inspire, and direct your audience as a fifth way to persuade and influence. Questions may engage your audience and challenge their opinions. Questions may also be used to get feedback, assess comprehension, and promote engagement. By asking your audience to visualize a situation, make a commitment, or voice their opinion, you may impact their behavior or attitude.

6. Use the power of metaphors

Metaphors, which connect two diverse things with something in common, are a sixth way to convince and influence your audience. Metaphors simplify complicated or abstract topics and generate vivid pictures or connections in your audience's mind. By appealing to emotions, generating contrast, or implanting a link or likeness, metaphors may convince and influence your audience. Use metaphors to relate your product, service, or concept to a buddy, guide, or solution your audience values, likes, or trusts.

Active Listening on a Deeper Level: Mining for Golden Nuggets

Networking encompasses more than mere business card exchanges and elevator presentations. It is about cultivating significant connections that contribute to personal and professional development. However, how can one accomplish this when encountering new individuals at conferences, events, or online platforms? Active attentiveness is among the most crucial abilities to possess. Active listening goes beyond mere reception of verbal communication. It entails demonstrating authentic curiosity, comprehending their viewpoint, and providing an appropriate reply.

1. Why active listening matters

Active listening demonstrates that you appreciate the other person's thoughts and the person you are conversing with. It also facilitates a deeper understanding of their objectives, obstacles, requirements, and passions. Doing so allows one to customize their communication to provide pertinent recommendations, guidance, or referrals. Additionally, it is possible to prevent misunderstandings, conflicts, and missed opportunities through active hearing. Through active listening, one can discern nuanced signals, request clarifications, and pose subsequent inquiries. Additionally, active listening can increase your memorability and likeability since others value those who attend to them.

2. How to prepare for active listening

Before initiating a conversation or attending a networking event, you must mentally prepare for active listening. This requires providing some open-ended inquiries, researching the individual or the subject, and establishing a clear purpose for the interaction. Additionally, you must eliminate from your mind any preconceived notions, biases, or diversions that could impede your ability to listen. Lastly, having a positive, curious disposition and a willingness to gain knowledge from others is essential.

3. How to demonstrate active listening

Through your verbal and nonverbal indicators, you must exhibit active listening during a conversation. Verbal signals consist of affirming, paraphrasing, summarizing, and pondering on the speaker's words. These strategies enable you to demonstrate comprehension, sympathy, and concurrence with them. In addition, they assist you in verifying accuracy and dispelling any uncertainties. Leaning forward, making eye contact, bowing, and beaming are all examples of nonverbal cues. Communicate your interest, engagement, and respect through these gestures. Additionally, they facilitate the development of rapport and trust.

4. How to respond to active listening

Following active listening, it is necessary to provide an appropriate response. This requires giving feedback, offering your viewpoint, and soliciting theirs. Maintaining honesty, respect, and constructiveness in your replies is also imperative. Avoid dominating, interrupting, or passing judgment on the conversation.

Attempt to establish common ground, provide value, and convey appreciation. You must also follow up with the individual via an invitation to interact further, a notation of appreciation, or a pertinent resource following the conversation.

5. How to improve your active listening skills

Like any other skill, active listening necessitates consistent practice and constructive feedback. You can enhance your listening abilities by applying active listening in various contexts, including formal and informal settings, offline and online platforms, and one-on-one and group discussions. Additionally, one may solicit feedback from others through direct inquiry or by observing their responses. One may also employ self-reflection and assessment instruments, including questionnaires, journals, or inventories, to evaluate one's strengths and deficiencies.

6. How to overcome challenges in active listening

Active listening can present difficulties, particularly in unfamiliar, boisterous, or congested environments. You may also encounter obstacles, including language, culture, or personality differences. Respectful, malleable, and adaptable behavior are required to surmount these obstacles. Additionally, it is imperative to employ tactics such as seeking clarification, repetition, or illustrative instances, using straightforward and uncomplicated language, and recognizing and resolving any uncertainties or disagreements. Additionally, you must be conscious of your emotions and inclinations and strive not to allow them to influence your listening.

Building Rapport: The Art of Instant and Deep Connection

Visualize entering a space and being immediately greeted by an individual who evokes feelings of understanding and connection. This is not mere chance; it is the skill of establishing rapport essential for developing robust and significant connections.

Building rapport is more than just a technique; it's crucial to establishing confidence and comprehension and a strong foundation for any personal, professional, or therapeutic relationship. This article explores the intricacies of establishing rapport and provides pragmatic advice and profound perspectives to improve one's capacity to develop genuine and efficient connections with others.

What is Rapport?

Rapport is a harmonious relationship characterized by effective communication and mutual understanding of one another's emotions and thoughts among the parties involved.

Components: A sense of connection, mutual respect, and comprehension.

The Importance of Building Rapport

- **In Personal Relationships:** Within the context of personal relationships, it fosters enhanced comprehension and more robust bonds.
- **In Professional Settings:** Promotes cooperation, collaboration, and effective communication in professional environments.
- **In Therapeutic Environments:** The critical element for fostering effective client-therapist relationships within therapeutic environments.

Steps to Build Rapport

- **Active Listening:** Demonstrate a genuine interest in the other person's words while paying complete attention to them.

- **Employing Mirroring Body Language:** Foster a sense of empathy by subtly imitating the other individual's posture, gestures, and expressions.
- **Establishing a Connection:** Consider identifying common interests or experiences to forge a bond.
- **Demonstrating Empathy:** Exhibit comprehension and compassion towards the viewpoint of another individual.
- **Open-Ended Questions:** Encourage deeper conversation and dialogue.

Overcoming Barriers to Rapport

- **Cultural Varieties:** Demonstrate cognizance and sensitivity towards cultural variations and standards.
- **Miscommunication:** Engaging in transparent and truthful communication is critical to surmount misunderstandings.
- **Personal Biases:** Recognize and set aside personal biases to foster genuine connections.

Enhancing Rapport through Emotional Intelligence

- **Self-Awareness:** Recognize the influence of one's emotions on interpersonal exchanges.
- **Self-Regulation:** To maintain a positive interaction, control your responses and reactions.
- **Social Skills:** Acquire negotiation, persuasion, and conflict resolution abilities.

The Lasting Impact of Rapport

Building rapport is a crucial ability that has the potential to revolutionize interactions and relationships. It is about fostering an environment characterized by mutual respect and comprehension in which genuine connections can thrive. By honing these abilities, we create opportunities for more gratifying and significant involvements across all spheres of life.

Advanced Persuasion Techniques: Forging Mutually Beneficial Collaborations

Possessing the capacity to convince prospective employers of your suitability for the position is equivalent to carrying a concealed weapon. You must possess the appropriate abilities, credentials, and accomplishments to demonstrate the value you will bring to a new company. However, mastering these persuasion techniques can be an absolute game-changer.

Before we continue, let's define persuasion and discuss various persuasion techniques. Persuasion consists of influencing an individual to take an action they would not typically take. Instead of attempting to exert control over an individual, your objective should be to introduce concepts and ideas in a manner that compels them to reconsider their position. Regarding your professional trajectory, persuasion entails demonstrating to the interviewing committee or recruiting manager that you possess the requisite qualifications to excel in the vacant position.

Top 5 persuasive techniques

Understanding the psychology underlying human decision-making and that decisions are rarely made based on pure logic are components of master persuasion. Even the most rational individuals rely on cognitive heuristics, biases, and emotions when determining how to proceed in a given circumstance. Consequently, understanding these psychological principles is vital.

1. **Reciprocity:** You are likely familiar with the adage, "A fly is easier to catch with honey than vinegar." The same holds regarding reciprocity. Individuals are more likely to respond positively when they anticipate receiving something in return for something they have contributed. Mentoring

novice colleagues and sharing industry insights at networking events are both examples of how reciprocity can be utilized.

2. **Social proof:** What is the initial step when making an online purchase? Are you a reader of reviews? Indeed, you do! This is because you desire assurance that others are undertaking the same endeavor you are undertaking and that they endorse it. Referrals and recommendations are the most effective means of capitalizing on social proof in the workplace. Additionally, it is advisable to obtain recommendations and endorsements for your LinkedIn profile.

3. **Authority:** By establishing connections with colleagues and discussing current events in your industry, you can establish yourself as an authority. Individuals are more receptive to being convinced to alter their positions if they perceive the individual requesting the change to be an authoritative figure with expertise in the subject matter.

4. **Liking:** People are more susceptible to being convinced to do something by those they trust, like, and know. If you invest effort in cultivating positive relationships with your coworkers and establishing rapport with them, you may gain access to opportunities such as promotions.

5. **Scarcity:** FOMO, which stands for "fear of missing out," has gained significant traction as an acronym on social media platforms due to its association with scarcity. An item or service becomes more desirable if a perception of scarcity can be generated. By instilling the recruiting manager with a sense of urgency, you can effectively leverage scarcity in an interview if you have taken the time to establish yourself as an authority in your field. They are more likely to employ you if they believe having an expert of your caliber on their

team could significantly improve the success of impending initiatives.

Summary

Achieving mastery of influence necessitates a nuanced equilibrium between assertiveness and regard for alternative perspectives. The text begins with examining the significance of active listening, an aptitude that transcends mere auditory perception by genuinely comprehending the implicit meanings conveyed. Such profound listening facilitates the identification of crucial insights, also known as "golden nuggets," which can be employed to establish meaningful connections with others.

The subsequent section of the chapter is devoted to rapport-building, the skill of establishing immediate and profound connections with others. The development of rapport is critical for successful persuasion, as it nurtures an atmosphere of confidence and acquaintance. People can rapidly establish connections with others by employing strategies such as mirroring, seeking areas of agreement, and utilizing positive body language. This segment offers pragmatic guidance on effectively establishing these connections across diverse contexts, including professional conferences and social assemblies.

The chapter concludes by discussing advanced persuasion techniques, emphasizing establishing mutually advantageous collaborations. Methods for effectively communicating concepts while highlighting the advantages for all involved are examined. The objective is to establish mutually beneficial situations that foster sustained collaboration and cooperation. By mastering these techniques, individuals can enhance their capacity to influence decisions, guide teams to success, and establish fruitful partnerships in their professional and personal spheres.

"Your network is your net worth." – Porter Gale

Chapter 3: Strategic Online Networking in the Virtual Frontier

Online networking and virtual conferences are a minefield. In this chapter we will delve into the complexities of networking in the contemporary digital era. By the end of this chapter you will have:

- **Optimize Your Profile**: Craft a compelling LinkedIn profile highlighting your professional achievements, skills, and experiences. Use a professional headshot, write a strong headline, and include a detailed summary to capture attention and establish credibility.
- **Build a Digital Brand**: Regularly share insightful content, industry news, and personal achievements to position yourself as a thought leader in your field. Engage with posts by liking, commenting, and sharing to increase visibility and build your brand.
- **Leverage Advanced Networking Strategies**: Utilize LinkedIn's advanced search and connection features to identify and reach out to key industry players, potential mentors, and collaborators. Personalize connection requests and follow up with meaningful conversations to cultivate strong professional relationships.
- **Engage in Virtual Networking Activities**: Participate in LinkedIn groups, webinars, and online events to expand your network and showcase your expertise. Actively contribute to discussions and offer valuable insights to engage effectively with peers and industry professionals.

Even with the prevalence of virtual interactions in the contemporary labor market, which is characterized by rapid change, the importance of networking must be emphasized. As individuals seeking employment traverse the digital realm in pursuit of fresh prospects, the significance of substantial connections has emerged as a critical factor in attaining professional prosperity. In the current age of online job searching, networking has evolved from a valuable supplement to an essential requirement.

Building Professional Relationships—Virtual networking transcends the traditional practice of exchanging business cards during in-person gatherings. Virtual events, online platforms, and professional social networks have emerged as contemporary domains where individuals establish and cultivate professional connections. By establishing connections with industry colleagues, potential mentors, and recruiters on platforms like LinkedIn, job seekers can access many career insights and cultivate a strong online presence.

Access to Hidden Opportunities—Many employment prospects are private but disseminated through professional networks. Such concealed opportunities can be accessed through networking. Increasing one's professional connections with industry experts can provide access to job opportunities that may need more publicity. Such insider knowledge may give you a distinct advantage in the employment market.

Showcasing Your Expertise—Online presence constitutes the initial impression in the digital realm. You can demonstrate your expertise via networking by engaging with others in your industry, actively participating in discussions, and sharing pertinent content. In addition to establishing your expertise as a thought leader, this increases your visibility to prospective employers interested in hiring individuals with your skills.

Adaptability and Resilience—In virtual employment, adaptability and resiliency are essential attributes that can be refined via networking. Interacting with professionals with a wide range of backgrounds provides opportunities for exposure to disparate viewpoints, industry developments, and career trajectories. The continuous evolution of industries and shifting job requirements render adaptability an invaluable asset.

Learning from Others—Besides facilitating career advancement, networking provides an opportunity to gain knowledge. Virtual networking events, webinars, and discussion forums serve as mediums to exchange knowledge, insights, and experiences. Engaging in these dialogues can provide significant insights that can augment your expertise and expand your comprehension of the field.

Overcoming Geographic Barriers—Virtual networking facilitates connecting with professionals worldwide, eliminating geographical constraints and enabling individuals seeking employment to investigate prospects outside their immediate vicinity. The prevalence of remote work has increased, and virtual networking provides access to a greater variety of opportunities.

Strengthening Personal Brand—Personal brands are precious assets in the current digital era. You can shape and fortify your brand through networking by demonstrating your competencies, accomplishments, and core values. A positive reputation is cultivated through consistent and genuine interactions with one's network, and this reputation can catalyze securing employment opportunities.

Virtual networking is not merely a practical alternative in the current labor market but an essential strategic necessity. Prospective employees who acknowledge the value of fostering significant relationships in the digital domain will have an advantage in navigating the ever-changing environment, gaining entry to concealed prospects, and constructing a versatile and robust professional trajectory. One should wholeheartedly adopt virtual networking and leverage their professional connections to propel themselves to success in the digital era.

Beyond Basics: Unleashing LinkedIn's Full Networking Potential

LinkedIn is an effective tool for professionals looking to develop a personal brand, find relevant connections, and look into employment opportunities. Although many users are acquainted with the fundamental features of LinkedIn, such as making a profile, requesting connections, and updating information, its true power is found in its sophisticated networking tools. Here's how you get the most out of LinkedIn and advance your networking.

- **Make Use of LinkedIn Groups**

LinkedIn Groups present a unique chance to network with other professionals who share your interests and with industry leaders. To get the most out of them, select groups based on industry, career interests, or professional objectives. Engage in active participation by posing queries, offering your ideas, and starting conversations. By doing this, you build your network and become recognized as an informed community member.

- **Make Your Profile as Visible as Possible**

Ensure your LinkedIn profile is optimized to draw in essential connections. Take a professional headshot and craft an attention-grabbing title highlighting your areas of expertise. Write a thorough synopsis that showcases your abilities, accomplishments, and experiences. Incorporate industry-specific keywords to increase search visibility. Having an optimized profile makes it more likely that recruiters and possible partners will find you.

- **Use the Search feature on LinkedIn to Locate Opportunities.**

LinkedIn's advanced search feature allows you to locate particular individuals, businesses, or employment openings. The filters allow you to focus your search on a specific industry, region, company size, and other factors. This function helps you find new career pathways, identify essential industry people, and make possible connections.

- **Use Strategic Content Engagement**

Creating content is only one aspect of developing a good LinkedIn profile; another is strategic engagement. Write fresh content highlighting your knowledge, share insightful articles, and leave comments on postings made by prominent sector members. Your reach grows, and new connections are drawn to you as you interact with other people's material and make yourself more visible to their networks.

- **Apply for Informational Interviews on LinkedIn**

One excellent approach to learning about other businesses, responsibilities, and career options is through informational interviews. LinkedIn is a great resource for connecting with professionals for these kinds of interviews. Write brief, customized notes outlining your goals for the connection and the information you hope to acquire. This strategy may yield insightful discoveries and even mentorship possibilities.

- **Make Use of LinkedIn Events and Learning**

There are many courses and tools available on LinkedIn Learning to help you improve your abilities. Engaging in these classes will help you learn more and build relationships with other students in the same courses. LinkedIn's event tool allows you to find and attend industry-related events, which opens up even more networking opportunities.

The full networking potential of LinkedIn extends far beyond creating profiles and requesting connections. Using the platform's sophisticated features, active participation in groups, profile optimization, and smart content engagement, you may build a strong network that leads to new business prospects and collaborative efforts. LinkedIn can be useful for professional development if you use it proactively.

Crafting a Captivating Digital Brand: Your Online Networking Magnet

Successful businesses in the current digital era must possess the capability to generate engaging content to establish a strong connection with their target audience. The need for exceptional digital content, ranging from thought-provoking blog posts to visually appealing social media updates, remains in high demand. How can one guarantee that their content distinguishes itself from the vast amount of online information?

Understanding Your Audience: The Key to Successful Content Creation

Before beginning the content creation process, it is vital to comprehend your intended audience thoroughly. Perform extensive research to ascertain the target audience's demographics, preferences, and challenges. You can increase engagement and resonance by customizing your content to address the specific concerns of your audience by gathering knowledge of their interests and requirements.

Embrace the Power of Storytelling

Audiences have always been captivated by the force of narratives, which holds true in the digital domain. Engaging audiences with captivating narratives has the potential to elicit emotions, cultivate connections, and create an enduring impact. Incorporating narratives into digital content, such as brand voyages, personal recollections, or customer success stories, enhances its authenticity and substance, increasing its memorability and relatability.

Optimize for Search Engines: Enhancing Discoverability

In a highly competitive digital environment, optimizing content for search engines is critical to increasing website discoverability and generating organic traffic. Perform keyword research to ascertain pertinent terms and phrases that are being sought after by your intended audience. Strategically incorporate keywords throughout your content: in headings, subheadings, meta descriptions, and secondary text. Enhancing the congruence between your content and pertinent search queries can augment your rankings in search engine results pages (SERPs) and draw more organic visitors.

Visual Appeal: Leveraging Multimedia Elements

By integrating multimedia components, including videos, images, infographics, and interactive elements, the visual allure of your digital content can be substantially improved. Visual aids facilitate comprehension by providing succinct breaks and enhancing the effectiveness of information transmission. Moreover, aesthetically pleasing content is more likely to capture the interest of its viewers and stimulate social sharing, thus expanding the scope of the content and magnifying its influence.

Engage Your Audience: Encourage Interaction and Feedback

Digital content operates on the lifeblood of engagement. Promote audience engagement and input by integrating interactive components into your content, including surveys, petitions, quizzes, and calls to action (CTAs). Solicit audience participation and discourse by extending invitations to like, share, and remark on your content across multiple platforms. Develop a sense of community and establish credibility with your audience by promptly and actively replying to comments and messages.

Measure and Iterate: Continuous Improvement

Iterative processes generate effective content. Use analytics tools to continuously monitor the efficacy of your digital content to determine what is and is not effective. To assess the effectiveness of your content, monitor engagement rates, click-through rates, page views, and conversion rates, among others. Leverage this data to enhance your content strategy, test novel methodologies, and optimize subsequent content to achieve superior outcomes.

Virtual Power Networking: Advanced Tactics for Online Engagement

Networking was frequently associated with physical gatherings, personal greetings, and the exchange of business cards. Nevertheless, the advent of the digital age has precipitated a paradigm shift in how we establish connections. The emergence of virtual networking has significantly altered the prevailing paradigm. The ascent of virtual networking is a reaction to the shifting work and communication environments, as opposed to merely a result of technological progress.

The necessity to physically attend conferences or meet-ups to broaden one's professional network is no longer applicable. Virtual networking has facilitated establishing connections among individuals, regardless of their geographical locations or cultural heritage. Engaging in a virtual conference in a foreign nation or participating in a panel discussion from the convenience of one's home office has introduced a novel aspect to the networking process.

Virtual private networking is progressing at an astounding rate. Constantly active social media platforms, online forums, and virtual events allow individuals to participate in networking endeavors at their preferred times and degrees. The advent of accessibility has revolutionized networking, establishing it as an uninterrupted and seamless process that transcends the limitations imposed by its time-limited nature.

Critical Components of Virtual Networking

Virtual networking is a complex domain with various essential elements that support establishing connections and collaborations in the digital space. Let us examine three critical elements that influence the experience of virtual networking:

- **Online Events and Platforms**

Virtual events and online platforms have emerged as the driving forces behind virtual networking. Digital centers offer platforms for professionals to gather, exchange knowledge, and establish relationships, all without the limitations imposed by geographical proximity. The migration of virtual seminars, panel discussions, and webinars from traditional conference rooms to our displays has provided individuals access to a wealth of information from any location. Participation in virtual events has been democratized through remote attendance, enabling individuals to engage with peers worldwide, gain insights from thought leaders, and participate in virtual events from the convenience of their environments.

- **Social Media and Professional Networks**

One can consider utilizing specialized professional networks and social media platforms as virtual networking event inspirations. Professionals can use industry-specific platforms like LinkedIn and Twitter to convene virtually to demonstrate their expertise, participate in dialogues, and form significant professional relationships. These platforms offer the means to broaden one's professional connections beyond conventional limits, facilitating exchanges that may result in partnerships, mentorships, and even pivotal opportunities in one's professional journey.

- **Webinars and Virtual Conferences**

Webinars and virtual conferences have emerged as dynamic platforms that facilitate the simultaneous exchange of knowledge and networking. These events allow attendees to gain knowledge from subject matter experts, participate in interactive discussions, and network with fellow attendees—all without having to deal with the logistical complexities associated with attending a physical event. Similar to in-person gatherings, webinars, and virtual conferences facilitate participant engagement through the ability to pose inquiries, exchange perspectives, and forge connections through the interactive nature of the platforms.

Summary

In Chapter 3 we learned about strategic online networking, an indispensable skill in the contemporary virtual realm. This chapter was about strategies for optimizing online platforms to establish meaningful connections and broaden one's professional influence. It begins with an in-depth examination of LinkedIn, guiding how to surpass the rudimentary aspects and fully exploit the capabilities of this platform. The emphasis is on profile optimization, strategic networking through LinkedIn's features, and community participation to establish a strong online presence. This segment offers recommendations for capturing the interest of prospective customers, recruiters, and industry frontrunners.

The subsequent section of the chapter is devoted to developing an engaging online brand that functions as a magnet for online networking. A robust digital brand can captivate individuals and create a lasting impact. This section underscores the significance of authenticity, consistency, and narrative construction when establishing a personal brand that effectively connects with the intended demographic. This course addresses approaches to effectively exhibit expertise, distribute valuable content, and establish oneself as an authority on various online platforms.

The chapter concludes by examining sophisticated strategies for virtual power networking. This process entails utilizing digital platforms to actively interact with individuals, even when in-person gatherings are unfeasible.

"Networking is more about farming than it is about hunting. It's about cultivating relationships." – Ivan Misner

Chapter 4: Commanding Attention: Public Speaking and Storytelling

How should we communicate to leave an effective positive lasting impression? In this chapter we will specifically look at how to:

- Acquire sophisticated public speaking abilities that will enable you to command attention at networking events
- Investigate the concept of proficient storytelling and convert your encounters into engrossing narratives that elicit a response from others.
- Unlock captivating communication strategies that elevate your capacity to establish meaningful connections with others and create unforgettable interactions.

Speaking in front of an audience can be a great way to inspire others, share ideas, and develop your brand. It provides a venue for deeper audience connection, inspiration, and influence. But the world of public speaking might appear overwhelming to those just starting. This will cover all the necessary advice for getting your first speaking engagement and give you an idea of what to expect financially.

Finding Your First Speaking Gig

1. Start by looking at local opportunities

The most straightforward approach to start speaking in front of an audience is to look for local possibilities. Think about joining Toastmasters clubs, community organizations, or local business groups. These platforms provide a stress-free setting for practice and confidence-boosting.

2. Make Use of Your Network

Make contact with friends, coworkers, and acquaintances who are participating in groups hosting gatherings or activities. Find out whether they are aware of any forthcoming speaking engagements. Making and maintaining connections through networking is essential to obtaining speaking engagements.

3. Create an Intriguing Subject

Choose a topic you are knowledgeable and passionate about speaking about. A distinctive approach can make you stand out to event organizers, whether your presentation is a personal narrative, a business case study, or an industry-specific insight.

4. Establish an Internet Identity

It is crucial to have an online portfolio that highlights your speaking experience and areas of expertise. Create an essential website or utilize LinkedIn to showcase your abilities, background, and speech subjects if you have them, and include audio or video recordings of your presentations.

5. Propose to event planners

After you've located conferences or events in your field of expertise, contact the hosts with a persuasive proposal. Provide a succinct bio, an overview of your subject, and any previous speaking engagements. Make it obvious to them what you have to offer and why your presentation will benefit them.

What to Expect Regarding Payment

1. Beginning: Low-Cost or Free Work

Many speakers start by giving free speeches to establish their credibility and gain experience. Small business groups, nonprofits, and local events frequently have tight resources, so be ready to provide your skills without charge. These first jobs, meanwhile, might be beneficial for networking and portfolio building.

2. Making the Switch to Paid Work

Once you have expertise and a reputation, speaking engagements can be charged. The event, the venue, and your level of experience all affect the rates. Fees for smaller events could be between $100 and $500. Speaking engagements for experienced speakers at larger conferences or business events pay anything from $1,000 to $10,000.

3. Negotiating Fees

Consider the event budget, travel expenditures, and preparation time when negotiating your speaking fee. It's crucial to look into the going prices for speakers in your sector or area. Be realistic about your expertise level and the value you bring, but don't be afraid to bargain.

4. Extra Reimbursement

Certain events may offer additional remuneration besides speaking fees, such as paying for your airfare and lodging, supplying meals, or letting you sell goods or services while you're there. Make careful to bring them up during negotiations, as they can significantly increase the value of your involvement.

Storytelling and public speaking can be immensely fulfilling both personally and professionally. With these pointers and strategies, you'll be well on your way to getting your first speaking engagement and establishing a lucrative public speaking career.

Owning the Stage: Advanced Public Speaking for Networking Events

People use public speaking to convey their thoughts or arguments to an audience, frequently to entertain or persuade others. This is a crucial ability because it enables speakers to establish rapport with their audience, which can assist them in influencing or inspiring their audience's actions or decisions. Acquiring knowledge regarding the advantages of public speaking can advance one's professional communication proficiencies.

1. Build your confidence

Developing one's confidence is possible via public speaking. Gaining knowledge on how to surmount any obstacles that may arise during the delivery of speeches could instill in you a sense of empowerment. Your confidence in speaking may be bolstered by the positive feedback you receive from moderators and audience members in the event of a successful performance. As you increase your amount of pre-speech practice, you may develop a greater sense of ease regarding the delivery and substance of your presentation.

2. Strengthen your critical thinking skills

Developing and delivering a speech necessitates introspection and analysis, which can be enhanced through public speaking. Creating a speech for an audience typically entails deliberating on the subject matter and organizing the speech accordingly. By employing critical thinking abilities, one can assess the reception of a speech by the audience and make an informed decision regarding whether to modify or sustain the delivery.

3. Expand your network

Delivering speeches at conferences and events can increase the size of your network. Following your speech, you may have the opportunity to connect with audience members from your industry. Additionally, you can establish connections with them after the event concludes via professional social networking platforms. Developing and sustaining connections with individuals within your professional network could potentially result in additional speaking engagements or career prospects.

4. Develop your leadership skills

Delivering a speech can enhance leadership abilities. It educates, entertains, or empowers the audience. By maintaining the attention of the audience and establishing yourself as a reliable purveyor of information, public speaking can aid in establishing credibility. These leadership abilities may apply to additional professional responsibilities, including presiding over group initiatives and meetings.

5. Use your performance skills

Public speaking can provide an opportunity to engage an audience from a platform or stage while utilizing one's performance abilities. Included among performance abilities are synchronization, cadence, and amplitude. For example, one can acquire the ability to discern when to employ deliberate pauses in discourse as a means of accentuating a specific aspect. To generate variety in your speaking, you can either speak more slowly or quickly or adjust the intensity of your voice.

6. Become a better listener

Participating in public discourse can enhance one's listening skills through constructive criticism provided after the speech. One can incorporate feedback into subsequent speeches or suggestions regarding subjects that interest the audience. As a public speaker, it is advantageous to observe the presentations of others and incorporate their effective elements into your forthcoming discourse. You could put your listening skills to use while conducting research for your speech by consulting a primary source.

Masterful Storytelling: Making Your Experiences Memorable

A prevalent misconception is that the narrative craft is an intricate and challenging endeavor best suited for a few proficient individuals. That is the furthest thing from the truth. Practicing the skills required to tell a story is possible; anyone with the proper equipment can become an expert storyteller.

Effective storytelling is crucial for engaging existing consumers or attracting new ones. Although visual media such as photographs and videos are included, the fundamental principles remain consistent.

1. Know your audience

This initial stage is critical as it will dictate the appropriate length of the story and the language that ought to be employed. Before you commence your story, devote five minutes to considering your audience.

Who are you conversing with? What is their age? What concerns them? Do they desire an extravagant experience or one that is affordable? Should you adopt a more formal demeanor, or would a cordial tone suffice? Does the publication intend to occur on Facebook, a blog post, or another platform?

These are critical elements to remember to establish an appropriate atmosphere and attain optimal results with your audience.

2. Make them care

Your audience must elicit an emotional, intellectual, or aesthetic response. This is crucial in a society where individuals frequently scan and disregard content cursorily.

Justify their interest in the narrative. What is its relevance to the target audience? Does your narrative address topics other than travel, including climate change, free speech, or sustainability?

Because if this is not crystal clear to you while constructing the narrative, it will not be crystal clear to the reader.

3. Be creative with chronology

Occasionally, to capture the reader's attention, you may immediately plunge them into the thick of the action or to the narrative's conclusion. Additionally, it is among the simplest methods for creating suspense, curiosity, and tension in a narrative. Due to the need for more clarity surrounding the situation, the reader will persist in reading to piece together the puzzle.

4. Know your punchline

What purpose does the narrative serve? It is crucial to remember that while your ultimate goal is to sell a product or service, the consumer should not perceive this as such. The narrative may possess comedic, sentimental, or a combination of these qualities; it might also be entirely distinct. While embracing creativity, it is crucial to maintain relevance and interest at all times.

5. Engage your audience

Raise the level playing field between the reader and the narrative. Incline them with one or two inquiries and position them as the narrative's focal point. By doing so, one generates an immediate and personal connection to the story, stimulating the reader's longing to partake in that particular experience for themselves.

6. End with a grand finale

Unless the narrative is intended to continue and suspense is deliberately built up, the story should have a resolution. Plot development should be complete, with no unanswered concerns remaining.

Incorporate enchantment into your narrative by evoking in your audience the same sense of wonder that you experience as you exit a magnificent movie theater. One method to accomplish this is to provide them with a "big question" concerning humanity or a comparable subject matter to contemplate during their return journey to their hotel.

Captivating Communication: Techniques for Unforgettable Networking

Effective communication is critical to the success of any networking effort. Irrespective of the setting (business conference, virtual rendezvous, local industry event, or social gathering), the efficacy of your communication skills can significantly impact the success or failure of your networking endeavors. This segment will delve into the intricacies of proficient communication concerning business networking. So you can see these techniques in action.

1. Active Listening: The Foundation of Effective Communication

Active listening as mentioned earlier in Chapter 2 involves more than mere auditory perception; it entails complete involvement with the speaker. Practice active listening during business networking by sustaining eye contact, nodding, and asking follow-up questions. Consider, for example, a networking event where an individual discusses their most recent undertaking. Instead of simply expressing recognition, further investigate it: "That is quite intriguing! In what manner did you surmount the technical obstacles?

Example: Sarah, a software engineer, attentively listens to Mark, an experienced entrepreneur, at a startup meetup. Mark provides an account of his trajectory from bootstrapping to obtaining venture capital. Sarah exhibits authentic interest by posing perceptive inquiries. Following her expression of gratitude, Mark connects her with prospective investors.

2. Clarity and Conciseness: Crafting Memorable Elevator Pitches

The time allotted to establish a good impression is frequently brief when engaging in networking activities. Your elevator speech ought to be succinct, distinct, and memorable. Remain focused on the value you deliver and avoid jargon. Specifically, "I specialize in data analytics, helping companies optimize their marketing strategies by analyzing customer behavior."

Example: The graphic designer Alex participates in a design conference. His succinct appeal—"I craft visually captivating narratives"—captivates the attention of other designers. As a result of exchanging business credentials, collaborative initiatives ensue.

3. Adaptability: Tailoring Your Message to Different Audiences

Effective communicators modify their tone, language, and content to fit the context. When networking, context should be considered. Are you conversing with a mentor, a fellow professional, or a prospective client? Adapt as necessary.

Example: A freelance writer, Maria, meets tech enthusiasts and literary agents at a writers' conference. She provides an overview of her content creation services to the latter while discussing her science fiction novel with the former.

4. Nonverbal Communication: Beyond Words

Intonating messages with your body language, facial expressions, and gestures is highly effective. A pleasant smile, a firm grasp, or an open posture effectively convey confidence and establish an approachable presence.

Example: Jake, a sales executive, participates in a trade show. His cordial disposition and firm palm shake contribute to a favorable perception. Potential consumers are at ease when conversing with him about business prospects.

5. Follow-Up Etiquette: Nurturing Connections

Effective communication transcends mere initial encounters. Deliver personalized follow-up messages via LinkedIn or email. To strengthen the connection, provide specific details from your conversation as references.

Example: A marketing manager, Emily, emails the guest speaker to express gratitude following a networking luncheon. They deliberate upon their mutual fascination with influencer marketing. The speaker replies, and a coffee conversation is arranged.

6. Digital Communication: Mastering email and Social media

In our globally interconnected society, digital communication is crucial. Produce expert-sounding emails, employ suitable subject lines, and conduct thorough proofreading. Build your online presence and engage meaningfully on social media by leaving comments and sharing valuable content.

Example: On Twitter, software developer David connects with his industry colleagues. By disseminating perceptive articles and engaging in pertinent discussions, he enhances his standing within the technological community.

Remember that effective communication depends not only on the content of your discourse but also on your expression. By refining your aptitude for communication, you will establish more robust relationships, unlock opportunities, and improve your standing in the networking community.

Summary

So, what have we learned? Throughout this chapter we have taken a deep dive into the critical skills of captivating an audience via narratives and public speaking, which are pivotal for effective networking. This chapter explores the intricacies of crafting compelling narratives and presentations that profoundly impact. The publication commences with a segment devoted to commanding attention, providing sophisticated public speaking methods customized specifically for networking occasions. Establishing a captivating presence requires an emphasis on self-assurance, vocal intonation, and body language. The reader is instructed on effectively managing anxiety and preparing for public speaking opportunities ranging from small networking gatherings to larger events.

We have look into how captivating communication techniques make networking unforgettable. These methodologies center around improving conversational aptitudes and include the implementation of active listening, mirroring, and open-ended questioning. The chapter guides the proficient use of humor, anecdotes, and personal insights to sustain vibrant and captivating discussions. The objective is to generate an enduring favorable perception among individuals, resulting in more substantial connections and networking opportunities. Through the skillful integration of public speaking, narrative, and captivating communication, individuals can command attention in any networking environment.

"Networking is the No.1 unwritten rule of success in business." – Sallie Krawcheck

Chapter 5: Strategic Relationship Building

Now, let's explore the importance of the establishment and sustenance of meaningful connections. Mapping your connections will teach you to network strategically, enabling you to identify crucial relationships and growth opportunities. Acquire knowledge and abilities that will allow you to easily navigate complex networks, manage dimensions of connections, and optimize networking endeavors. Investigate strategies for fostering deeper connections to establish enduring, mutually advantageous relationships, thereby guaranteeing the continuity of a robust and supportive network.

Successful networking initiatives revolve around building strategic relationships. This chapter explores essential methods and approaches for building lasting connections that may advance your professional development.

- **Determine Your Networking Objectives:** Establishing clear networking objectives is essential before launching into connection building. A clear understanding of your goals will direct your efforts and concentrate on the most relevant connections, whether you want to explore employment options, seek mentoring, or grow your professional network.

- **Research and Target:** Targeted research is the foundation for strategic connection building. Find people or groups who share your objectives and passions, and then learn more about their experiences, backgrounds, and specializations. Adjust your strategy and build a better rapport immediately by knowing their requirements and priorities.

- **Offer Value:** Reciprocity is a fundamental component of strategic relationship building. Give value to the people you connect with by helping them or offering advice or resources that help them overcome obstacles. By exhibiting your readiness to participate and provide value, you establish the groundwork for a partnership that benefits both parties.

- **Create Sincere Connections:** Relationship building requires authenticity above all else. Be sincere, empathetic, and interested in getting to know the other person while exchanging. Establishing a relationship based on trust, respect, and similar values should be your primary focus while building rapport.

- **Maintain Consistent Communication:** Constant involvement and communication are necessary for effective relationship building. Maintain frequent communication with your contacts by sending emails, making phone calls, or holding meetings. Over time, look for chances to re-establish and strengthen your relationship. Relationships are strengthened and maintained when there is consistent communication between the parties.

- **Attend Networking Events:** These gatherings provide priceless chances to make new friends and widen your network. Participate in industry conferences, seminars, and workshops to network with like-minded individuals, share ideas, and consider joint ventures. Be the one to discuss and introduce yourself to new people.

- **Follow-Through and Follow-Up:** Building a relationship requires following up. Send a customized follow-up note after the first meetings or exchanges to show gratitude and strengthen the relationship. Keep your pledges or commitments throughout the discussion to gain credibility and confidence.

- **Seek Mentorship and Guidance:** Mentoring is among the most effective career advancement and development strategies. Look for mentors who can provide career guidance, advice, and support. Make a proactive effort to connect with possible mentors and convey your desire to gain knowledge from their experiences.

- **Provide Support and Assistance:** Relationship building is a two-way street, so provide support and assistance. Whenever you can, help and support your relationships. This might be lending a sympathetic ear, giving resources, or making recommendations. By being willing to assist others, you strengthen the relationship and promote a reciprocity-based society.

- **Evaluate and Nurture Relationships:** Evaluate your relationships to ensure they align with your values and goals. Identify those that may no longer support your goals and devote time and energy to cultivating worthwhile and advantageous connections between both parties. Put all your effort into developing relationships that will help you succeed professionally.

One of the critical components of successful networking is building strategic relationships. You can establish a robust network of connections that will support your career aspirations and long-term success by establishing clear goals, carrying out focused research, providing value, fostering real connections, staying in constant communication, going to networking events, following up, looking for mentorship, offering support, assessing and building relationships.

Networking with Intention: Mapping Your Connections

Networking can be daunting, and learning how to do it correctly and intentionally is challenging.

Before delving into the networking dos and don'ts, it is imperative to define networking.

Interacting with others to exchange information and establish professional or social connections constitutes networking.

Although challenging, achieving the ideal equilibrium is undeniably an art form. However, we have the DOs and DON'Ts to guarantee your networking is productive and worthwhile!

Do

- **Act Transparently**

Feel free to seek advice and guidance whenever necessary. If you are courteous and forthright about your intentions, people will want to assist you.

- **Understand Boundaries**

Acknowledge instances where the other individual fails to provide timely responses or offers frank responses, and come to the understanding that maintaining friendships with all is unattainable. Keep in mind that maintaining a selective inner circle is significantly more productive.

- **Accommodate**

There is nothing worse than requesting assistance on your own terms without considering what you are offering in return. Ask them what would be most convenient, and be flexible enough to modify your plans accordingly.

Don't

- **Be Unprepared**

That relationship will only develop if you begin a conversation with the correct person's name or if it is evident that you have yet to do your research. Otherwise, that encounter will be remembered by others and will only harm your reputation.

- **Be Overly Vague**

It is useless to say, "Hello, I need your assistance promoting my brand," without providing additional information. Be Particular. To illustrate, you might say, "Hello!" I hope you can assist me in expanding the reach of my brand, mainly through email marketing and SEO...

- **Give Less and Take More**

It is unfair to demand gratuitous contributions of others' time and effort. While requesting a favor may occasionally be effective, ensuring that you are providing something in return is critical. For instance, offer them a discount on your upcoming masterclass or assist with their brand design. It is unnecessary to be enormous, but it makes a significant impact!

Navigating Complex Networks: Strategies for Multi-Dimensional Connection

Is your networking purposeful? Most individuals initiate networking as a trial run. Typically, they are invited by a friend or colleague, after which they establish themselves, forge a few meaningful connections, and potentially generate some business. However, the occasion is more of a social gathering, with the option to depart as soon as business resumes. Networking with purpose and a predetermined objective in mind elevates the experience to an entirely new level and requires an entirely different mentality. This is what I want for you as a Networking Master - you should network deliberately:

- Clarify your networking goals.
- Identify your target connections.
- Plan your approach to build rapport.
- Decide what you will contribute to the relationship.
- Define your expectations for the relationship.
- Ensure mutual benefit within your network.

By approaching networking from a state of intention and knowledge, one can broaden one's perspective. We adopt a distinct perspective on networking, regarding it as a chance to expand our social circle by introducing others. We actively seek opportunities and networks that contribute to our professional and personal development.

Determine with purpose where, how, and when you will conduct your networking. Decide deliberately on whom you will pursue, how you will conduct follow-up, and how much time you will devote to cultivating relationships with the individuals in your network. Determine your network objectives and the effort you will invest to achieve them.

What do you want...

- More business?
- More referrals?
- Stronger partnerships?
- Increased social interaction?
- Enhanced learning?
- Greater media exposure?
- More speaking opportunities?
- Engaging conversations?

When you have a clear understanding of your objectives, you will be capable of responding to connections who inquire about how they can assist you. Let your network assist you with whatever you require assistance with; it is essentially about assisting one another.

- Evaluate your network members and your rapport with them.
- Plan future collaborations for the next year.
- Assess your effort in maintaining the network.

- Ensure your network understands your work and how you help clients.
- Check if they help you find clients.
- Ensure you help them find their clients.
- Confirm they have the right connections to support your growth.

If most of these queries have been answered negatively, it may be time to consider switching networks. That is fine! Occasionally, our business requirements change, or we exceed our network to the point where we no longer connect in the appropriate locations. Be adaptable in your approach to conducting business and seek out new connections.

Most critical: Act deliberately toward serving others without anticipation of reciprocation; maintain an optimistic yet non-expectant attitude. As a result, socializing and networking are significantly more enjoyable.

Deepening Connections: Strategies for Long-Term, Mutually Beneficial Relationships

Networking entails more than simply adding contacts or exchanging business credentials. It involves establishing connections with significance that can facilitate the expansion of your brand and generate prospects for cooperation, knowledge acquisition, and reciprocal assistance. Achieving mutually beneficial partnerships through networking can be achieved by adhering to the subsequent five steps:

1. Determine your objectives and values

Before you begin networking, you must have a clear understanding of your objectives and personal stance. Your objectives and principles will provide direction in identifying suitable individuals to engage with and in articulating your distinct value proposition. For example, in the pursuit of expanding one's knowledge regarding a particular field or aptitude, one may seek out individuals possessing pertinent expertise or experience. Potential collaborators may be interested in your skills or resources if your core value is to assist others.

2. Investigate and seek out

After identifying your values and objectives, you can initiate research and contact potential partners. Through interactions at events, online platforms, publications, social media, or referrals, you may locate individuals who possess similar interests, obstacles, or ambitions. Subsequently, you may commence communication by means of a customized electronic mail, invitation, or message that demonstrates authentic inquiry and interest. Avoid sending spammy or generic communications solely about you or your agenda.

3. Developing rapport and trust

Once communication has been established, developing rapport and trust with potential collaborators is essential. This can be accomplished through open-ended inquiries, meaningful dialogue, attentive listening, empathy, and conversation. In addition, one may contribute anecdotes, insights, or feedback while also recognizing the accomplishments, obstacles, or viewpoints of others. The objective is to establish a profound connection that transcends superficiality and demonstrates concern for the individuals involved.

4. Request and offer value

Additionally, as rapport and trust are established, prospective partners can be asked to provide and accept value. Value can encompass anything that assists the other party or both parties in attaining their objectives, including endorsements, information, counsel, referrals, and introductions. Offering value first, without expecting anything in return, and requesting value respectfully and specifically are crucial. One may also convey appreciation and gratitude for their assistance and, if feasible, reciprocate.

5. Preserve and cultivate the relationship

The ultimate phase entails fostering and preserving the bond between one's companions. One can accomplish this by maintaining consistent communication, following up on discussions, offering assistance, sharing pertinent resources, providing updates, and sharing relevant resources. One may also seek opportunities to collaborate on initiatives, attend events, meet in person, or join online communities. The objective is to maintain a mutually beneficial relationship for all involved.

Summary

Great Job on completing Chapter 5! You're halfway there!

This chapter focused on strategic relationship building, highlighting the importance of purposeful networking and organized connections. The chapter began with mapping your connections, stressing the need to understand your professional network's landscape. By creating a detailed network map, you can identify potential collaborators, key stakeholders, and growth opportunities. The provided frameworks and tools help visualize these networks, allowing for a more systematic approach to networking.

Next, the chapter explored methods for managing complex networks. As networks grow, they become more multidimensional, spanning various industries and interests. This section offered strategies for balancing and organizing these intricate networks. Readers learned how to interact effectively with diverse individuals, build rapport, and foster understanding among different groups.

The goal is to create a resilient network that can thrive in changing conditions.

The chapter also discussed ways to strengthen connections and build long-lasting, mutually beneficial partnerships. It emphasized authentic connections over superficial interactions. Key points included the importance of consistent communication, providing value to others, and maintaining authenticity. Techniques for gradually nurturing relationships were examined to ensure they remain strong and beneficial. By applying these strategies, readers can build a reliable network that supports their personal and professional goals.

"All the time and effort put into networking can be all for nought if there is no follow-through. The same goes for sales. And leadership. And well, everything." – Beth Ramsay

Chapter 6: High-Level Engagement and Executive Networking

Ok - now we are going to focus on cultivating connections with industry executives and leaders. Throughout this chapter you will:

- Gain the ability to confidently approach industry leaders, facilitating the formation of significant connections at the highest echelons.
- Master sophisticated methods for cultivating connections within the C-suite, enabling you to navigate high-level networking adeptly.
- Investigate methods for obtaining mentorship from industry pioneers who are also leaders in your field, utilizing their knowledge and expertise to advance your career and leadership growth.

Networking is an indispensable component in the contemporary professional environment. It facilitates access to prospects and nurtures individual and vocational development.

Establishing connections with influential individuals can have a transformative effect on professional networking.

These prominent individuals have access to invaluable knowledge, connections, and insights that can significantly advance your career. However, maneuvering through networking with influential individuals necessitates tact and a calculated methodology.

Presenting the Problem:

Effective networking with influential individuals is difficult because they are frequently inundated with requests and encircled by a network of established connections. Unplanned or haphazard approaches may result in missed opportunities and a dearth of significant connections. Moreover, the apprehension of appearing opportunistic or lacking sincerity may impede people from capitalizing on these prospective connections.

A Professional Efficient Approach in 6 Steps:

Research and Select Strategically:

Before networking with influential individuals, it is essential to identify and investigate potential connections meticulously. Gain insight into their specialized knowledge, personal interests, and the sectors in which they operate. Use online platforms, industry events, and mutual connections for information gathering. After amassing a roster of prospective contacts, arrange them in order of importance about your objectives and shared passions.

Create Value Before Seeking It:

It is common to approach influential people with requests for their time and aid. Establishing one's uniqueness requires providing value before expecting anything in return. This may entail disseminating thought-provoking material, furnishing pertinent data, or establishing connections to invaluable resources. Establishing a foundation of reciprocity through demonstrating your willingness to contribute to their professional network can facilitate the development of a more meaningful relationship.

Build Genuine Relationships:

In networking, authenticity is crucial, particularly when interacting with influential individuals. Demonstrate a sincere interest in people's endeavors and accomplishments when interacting. Participate in online forums, attend industry events, and engage in discussions where these individuals are prominent. It takes time to build relationships, so exercise patience and concentrate on fostering a bond based on shared values and objectives.

Utilize Warm Introductions:

Utilize the connections you have established to obtain cordial introductions to influential individuals. A cordial introduction facilitated by a mutual acquaintance increases your likelihood of being acknowledged and considered substantially. Communicate with acquaintances, mentors, colleagues, sector insiders, alliance partners, or associates who might have relationships with the targeted individuals. In your introduction, specify your intentions and why you believe it would be mutually beneficial.

Follow Up Strategically:

Sustained and calculated follow-up is critical for fostering and preserving relationships with influential individuals. After an initial encounter or meeting, communicate your gratitude for their time through a personalized thank-you message. Periodically provide updates regarding your progress or common interests. This practice strengthens your dedication to the partnership while maintaining their attention.

Build Your Reputation as a Thought Leader:

An imperative further measure in cultivating connections with influential individuals is proactively establishing yourself as a preeminent authority in your field. Impart your knowledge through panel discussions, conferences, blog posts, articles, and social media. By consistently providing insightful observations and unique perspectives, one not only builds credibility but also garners the interest of influential individuals who value and actively pursue leaders in their respective industries. Establishing oneself as a thought leader increases prominence and renders oneself a highly sought-after professional.

Networking with Industry Titans: Approaching Leaders with Confidence

Professionals have a rare chance to network with powerful executives with a wealth of knowledge and insights into their respective professions by connecting with industry giants. While it could seem intimidating to approach these people, doing so confidently can result in insightful conversations, worthwhile contacts, and mentoring possibilities that can further one's career.

Confidence is crucial when networking with business giants. It's critical to enter these exchanges with equality and respect, understanding that you, too, have important insights and things to contribute. Approach industry leaders as peers rather than superiors, and have faith in the worth of your experiences, knowledge, and suggestions.

It's essential to be ready before meeting with industry heavyweights. Investigate their experience, qualifications, and areas of specialization. Recognize their career path and any current endeavors or projects they have participated in. You may create a meaningful connection by showing that you are genuinely interested in their accomplishments and work area.

Communicate straightforwardly and concisely while corresponding with powerful people in the business. Write a customized note that conveys your desire to contact them and emphasizes how much you like their work. Elucidate the benefits you can provide by exchanging knowledge, looking for a mentor, or looking into possible joint ventures. You may project professionalism and regard for their time by making your aims and goals apparent.

A sincere connection and rapport-building are the main goals of networking with powerful people in the sector. Pay close attention to what they have to say and participate in the discussion by actively hearing their opinions. Be receptive to learning from their experiences and show interest and curiosity by asking meaningful questions. You can establish a good rapport and form the foundation for a successful relationship by asking questions and expressing gratitude for their expertise.

Connecting with powerful people in the business allows you to share your knowledge and perspectives. Give examples of your achievements, experiences, and viewpoints that highlight your worth and area of expertise in your profession. Be specific when expressing your thoughts and beliefs, and be ready to participate in thoughtful conversations about subjects that both of you find interesting. By demonstrating your skills and experience, you set yourself up as a valued resource and possible partner.

Networking with powerful people in the field is crucial while maintaining your integrity and modesty. Be truthful about your personal background, assets, and room for improvement. Recognize with humility that there is always more to learn, and be receptive to advice and criticism from prominent figures in the field. Your relationships with powerful businesspeople are strengthened when you exhibit sincerity and humility.

Networking with powerful people in the field demands self-assurance, planning, and persistence. By exhibiting humility, genuineness, and respect in these conversations, professionals may establish significant bonds with powerful leaders that significantly influence their future career path. Networking with industry titans may lead to new possibilities, mentoring, and insights that can propel professional progress and success if done with the correct attitude and approach.

Establishing C-Suite Connections: Advanced Techniques for High-Level Networking

A crucial element of both personal and professional development is networking. Additionally, an individual's values, priorities, and interests are reflected in their network. Life-shaping influences are companions and acquaintances, which begin in early infancy. "Show me your friends, and I will tell you who you are," said Dan Pena. Lifelong networking is dynamic and iterative. Maintaining a network at C-level efficiency necessitates continual learning and reciprocity. In a time-constrained environment, targeted networking is critical. Nevertheless, it is crucial to recognize the significance of expanding one's horizons to hear and assimilate knowledge from diverse sectors and areas of interest.

Reestablishing a foundational approach to network development entails refocusing attention on the following:

- Reciprocity
- Purposeful network authentication
- Utilization of an operational system
- Intellectual growth through continuous education

1. Reciprocating

Demonstrating generosity is of the utmost importance in the context of networks. Harvey Mackay, founder, CEO, and best-selling author, asserts, "In the absence of reciprocity, one may appear extremely self-centered and sever ties with one's network." Dedicate your complete attention to the dependable relationships cultivated through diligence, perseverance, and time investment.

Effective reciprocity requires C-suite executives to be receptive to and cognizant of their contacts' interests and requirements. When requesting a favor, one must contemplate methods of reciprocating that favor. Reciprocity is fundamental to establishing significant and influential relationships.

2. Authenticity

The foundation of authenticity in a network is intent. Determine subject matters or domains in which a significant influence can be exerted. Is it possible to form circles of influence to achieve shared objectives? Paul Polman, the former CEO of Unilever and the individual credited with driving the company's transition towards a net positive balance, ardently supports purpose-driven networking. "On the verge of achieving true scale and velocity, nations and industries require audacious alliances." Polman defines his objective in his statement, which refers to the necessity of collaboration as forming partnerships with organizations that can assist in fulfilling the same commitment he made to Unilever.

3. Keeping track

Establishing an authentic network requires time and effort and can frequently divert a CXO's focus from other critical responsibilities. With a method for organizing contacts and pertinent information about them, it is easier to allocate time for family, acquaintances, and significant others.

A career coach for Korn Ferry Advance, Val Olson, emphasizes the importance of maintaining records of the interests and specifics of one's contacts. "By following up with the individual the following time, you can inquire about the progress of their recently adopted pastime of ocean swimming or forward them an article pertinent to the subject matter you discussed." A C-suite executive must prioritize identifying a platform that facilitates the effective monitoring of contacts, including their professional activities, personal interests, and interests.

4. Widening the lens

To broaden one's horizons, one must venture beyond one's comfort zone and investigate uncharted knowledge domains. A network of contacts can assist in expanding one's horizons by introducing organizations and activities that other C-suite executives are pursuing. Exploration of these interests generally transpires via informal pursuits such as participation in wine societies, cycling, trekking, golfing, and engaging in art and culture. The cultivation of relationships occurs via exchanging anecdotes, ideas, thoughts, and perseverance throughout engagements and activities.

5. Join a CxO peer group

Peer organizations provide an excellent opportunity to access a wide range of knowledge domains and a more elevated perspective on areas of shared expertise. Managing a business can cause one to lose sight of their interests. At times, the only person who can comprehend or empathize with the difficulties faced by an executive may be another executive. Thankfully, CxO peer groups exist to provide valuable support, constructive criticism, emotional encouragement, and access to new opportunities.

Learning from the Best: Gaining Mentorship from Industry Pioneers

Mentoring is a potent instrument that can significantly impact a person's success in business networking. Building and maintaining professional relationships is critical for developing and succeeding in a competitive environment. Even with this, novices or those with the requisite expertise may find it particularly difficult to navigate the intricacies of business networking.

In such situations, mentorship becomes significant. Mentors can facilitate personal and professional development by aiding individuals in navigating the complexities of business networking through providing guidance, support, and knowledge. This, in turn, can lead to the discovery of new opportunities.

The Role of Mentorship in Nurturing Professional Relationships

Mentorship is an indispensable component in fostering professional connections within business networking. A mentor is an individual who possesses prior success in their respective domain and is eager to impart their expertise, experience, and perceptions to a protégé. The assistance and encouragement provided can be very valuable in aiding people through the intricacies of establishing and sustaining professional connections.

The following are some methods by which mentoring fosters professional relationships:

1. **Providing guidance and insights:** Mentors possess the ability to impart invaluable guidance and insights derived from their personal experiences, thereby aiding mentees in maneuvering through arduous circumstances, formulating well-informed judgments, and circumventing prevalent pitfalls.

2. **Network expansion:** Mentors frequently possess vast professional networks and can facilitate connections between mentees and influential individuals, granting access to novel prospects and collaborative ventures.

3. **Providing constructive feedback:** In order to assist mentees in honing their networking abilities, communication aptitude, and overall professional comportment, a mentor may offer candid and constructive feedback.

4. **Serving as a sounding board:** Mentors can provide a secure environment where mentees can openly exchange thoughts, obstacles, and ambitions, thereby offering a novel viewpoint and aiding mentees in attaining a clear understanding of their objectives and priorities.

5. **Fostering self-assurance:** Mentors can assist mentees in expanding their professional networks and overcoming uncertainties by offering encouragement, support, and validation. This, in turn, empowers mentees to cultivate and maintain professional connections more efficiently.

How Can Mentorship Enhance Networking Skills and Strategies?

Mentorship is paramount in developing networking abilities and tactics, enabling individuals to maneuver through the intricacies of business connections more adeptly. This paper examines several methods by which mentorship can aid in the growth and improvement of networking abilities.

- **Learning From Real-Life Examples**

Mentors can impart practical insights and actionable advice to mentees, giving them real-life illustrations of effective networking strategies and their own experiences. Mentors who have achieved networking success can teach mentees about effective and ineffective strategies for establishing and sustaining professional relationships.

- **Role-Playing And Practice**

Mentors can simulate authentic networking situations with mentees through role-playing exercises. This provides a secure and encouraging setting for mentees to enhance their networking abilities while receiving constructive criticism and direction from their mentor. Through role-playing, mentees can hone their communication skills, gain self-assurance, and surmount any apprehensions or obstacles they might encounter while engaging in networking activities.

- **Strategies And Action Plans That Are Tailored**

Mentorship can assist mentees in formulating action plans and networking strategies tailored to their aspirations and objectives. By gaining a comprehension of the mentee's distinct circumstances, sector, and goals, mentors can offer customized counsel and direction that aligns with the mentee's particular requirements.

- **Feedback And Ongoing Enhancement**

Mentors can offer insightful criticism regarding the mentee's networking endeavors, thereby assisting the latter in pinpointing areas that require enhancement and honing their strategy. Mentees are consistently coached and developed using this feedback cycle, and their networking strategies are modified to yield superior outcomes as time passes.

- **Developing Self-Assurance And Conquering Obstacles**

Networking can be daunting, especially for individuals who are inexperienced or new to the industry. Mentors can assist mentees in overcoming obstacles and gaining self-assurance through encouragement, support, and direction. Mentors help mentees overcome typical networking anxieties and concerns, encouraging them to venture beyond their comfort zones and establish significant connections.

Summary

So, what exactly have we learned in this chapter?

Chapter 6 presents an in-depth analysis of executive networking and high-level engagement, offering guidance on establishing connections with industry leaders and executives

The chapter underscores the critical importance of networking with influential figures and equips readers with techniques to confidently approach executives.

The chapter begins by examining the necessary mentality and readiness for interacting with influential individuals. It advises on conducting thorough research on leaders, determining priorities, and identifying shared interests to foster meaningful dialogues. By adopting a confident demeanor and showing genuine curiosity, readers can form solid relationships with key industry players.

The next section explores sophisticated strategies for establishing connections within the C-suite. It emphasizes the significance of nurturing relationships with executives and decision-makers. Practical advice is provided on finding opportunities to engage with top executives through professional organizations, industry events, and other networking avenues. The section also covers effective communication strategies tailored for high-level engagements, focusing on succinctly presenting ideas and leaving a lasting impression. Readers learn how to position themselves as valuable resources for senior professionals.

The chapter concludes with a focus on mentorship from industry pioneers. It highlights mentorship as a powerful tool for professional growth and offers strategies for approaching potential mentors and building substantial connections with them. The importance of receiving guidance from experienced practitioners is emphasized, along with tips for maintaining a productive mentor-mentee relationship. Readers are guided on how to find suitable mentors, set clear objectives, and express gratitude for the mentorship they receive.

By implementing the strategies outlined in this chapter, you can gain access to invaluable insights and knowledge from industry leaders, paving the way for greater professional success.

"The richest people in the world build networks. Everyone else is trained to look for work." – Robert Kiyosaki

Chapter 7: Networking Across Cultures and Borders

In this chapter, you will learn an examination of the requisite competencies and tactics that govern successful international networking. Gain cultural intelligence to thrive in global interactions; learn to navigate the complexities of different cultures and communication styles. Explore sophisticated cross-border networking tactics that facilitate the formation of resilient global connections, thereby augmenting one's sphere of impact and visibility. Finally, attained expertise in formulating international alliances, acquiring knowledge on prospering in varied business settings, and forging enduring cross-cultural collaborations.

In today's globalized world, networking across cultural and geographical boundaries is crucial for anyone hoping to increase their effect and influence. In today's globally interconnected world, the capacity to form deep connections across cultural divides can lead to exceptional chances, creative teamwork, and a broader perspective on the world. However, navigating nuanced cultural differences, adjusting to various communication styles, and cultivating sincere connections that cut beyond national lines are all necessary for networking successfully in a cross-cultural setting.

- **Establish Authenticity to Gain Trust**

Establishing trust is essential for cross-cultural networking. Building credibility requires honesty and a sincere interest in the individuals you meet. This entails paying attention to their cultural backgrounds, listening intently, and avoiding generalizations. Establishing common ground via similar professional experiences, interests, or objectives is a useful strategy for fostering trust. Once trust is built, cross-cultural connections can thrive and develop into deeper collaborations and partnerships.

- **Utilize Technology to Close Gaps**

Cross-border networking is now easier than ever, thanks to technology. Professionals can make real-timers can make Real-tools such as Slack, Zoom, and LinkedIn. Technology may, however, overcome geographical barriers, so it's essential to use it carefully. Attention to preferred communication mediums, cultural holidays, and time zone differences. A sophisticated networking mindset considers these elements to guarantee smooth communication and deep connections.

- **Develop a Global Perspective**

To network across cultural boundaries, it's critical to develop a global perspective. This entails seeking cross-cultural encounters, accepting diversity, and remaining receptive to novel concepts. Participating in foreign projects, attending conferences abroad, and being a member of multicultural networking groups can all help you broaden your horizons and open your eyes. A global perspective promotes adaptation and never-ending learning, two essential qualities for effective cross-cultural networking.

Cultural Intelligence in Networking: Excelling in Global Connections

Success in international networking activities greatly depends on cultural intelligence or CQ. Understanding and adjusting to cultural differences becomes crucial for building effective cross-border partnerships as professionals negotiate more varied and linked corporate environments.

Comprehending Cultural Dynamics

To succeed in global networking, professionals must first comprehend workplace cultural dynamics. This entails acknowledging that many cultural groups have unique conventions, beliefs, communication methods, and behavioral patterns. By grasping these subtle cultural differences, people better handle cross-cultural encounters and prevent misunderstandings. Furthermore, professionals may adjust their approach and communication style to connect with people from different cultural backgrounds by being thoroughly aware of the cultural environment.

Raising Cultural Intelligence

Improving cultural intelligence begins with developing cultural awareness. Professionals need to learn about the social norms, practices, traditions, and beliefs of the cultures they work with. This might involve taking part in cultural sensitivity training courses, reading books, articles, and research papers on intercultural communication, or asking mentors with cross-cultural experience for advice. Broadening their cultural knowledge may foster empathy and an understanding of other viewpoints, which paves the way for fruitful international networking.

Modifying Communication Approaches

Changing communication styles is necessary for cross-cultural networking to be successful. Professionals should consider language hurdles, nonverbal clues, and environmental variations since they may affect communication. They should speak succinctly and avoid slang or jargon that others from other cultural backgrounds may need to learn. Professionals should also be aware of nonverbal communication indicators, such as body language and facial expressions, which might differ depending on the culture. Professionals from varied backgrounds may develop rapport and promote mutual understanding by modifying their communication style to account for cultural variations.

Adopting Cultural Empathy

Developing cultural intelligence in networking requires embracing cultural humility. Admitting cultural prejudices, constraints, and presumptions and approaching cross-cultural relationships with an open mind and a desire to learn are all parts of cultural humility. Professionals should have a modest attitude, understanding that cultural competency is a lifelong process and that they may not have all the answers. They should also be receptive to advice and criticism from people with different experiences and see every contact as a chance for professional and personal development. Professionals adopting cultural humility may promote cooperation, mutual respect, and understanding in international networking initiatives.

Making the Most of Diversity

Regarding networking, professionals need to use diversity to their advantage. Cultural differences should be seen as possibilities for innovation, creativity, and progress rather than barriers. By integrating people with varying viewpoints, experiences, and knowledge, professionals may foster creativity in global networking, solve intricate challenges, and provide fresh ideas. Furthermore, a diversified network makes it easier for people to access a wider variety of opportunities, contacts, and resources, which improves their capacity to meet their professional goals and objectives.

Cultural knowledge is a must for success in international networking. Professionals may improve their capacity to handle cross-cultural encounters effectively by understanding cultural dynamics, cultivating cultural awareness, adjusting communication methods, building rapport and trust, accepting cultural humility, and using diversity as a strength. Professionals with a high degree of cultural intelligence may succeed in today's more interconnected world by fostering meaningful connections and teamwork.

Building International Networks: Advanced Cross-Border Strategies

In the current era characterized by the globalization of business, cultural intelligence has become an indispensable competency for individuals involved in international business. In this analysis, we shall explore the notion of cultural intelligence and ascertain its criticality in achieving triumph in the global business arena.

Definition of Cultural Intelligence (CQ): Cultural intelligence (CQ) transcends mere cultural consciousness. It represents the capacity to navigate and engage with individuals of various cultures productively, cultivating significant connections and appreciating a range of viewpoints. A considerable degree of cultural intelligence is a game-changing quality in the realm of international business.

Four Elements Constituting Cultural Intelligence:

1. ***CQ Drive:*** Intrinsic Motivation: Culturally savvy people are intrinsically motivated to develop an appreciation and comprehension of diverse cultures. This intrinsic motivation fosters an authentic curiosity and admiration for diversity. Self-assurance: Professionals with a high CQ drive exhibit self-assurance when engaging in intercultural interactions, empowering them to confront unfamiliar circumstances with an optimistic and flexible mindset.

2. ***CQ Knowledge:*** Cultural Systems Awareness: It is fundamental to comprehend various societies' cultural norms, values, and practices. Beyond superficial understanding, this subject necessitates a profound comprehension of the historical and social milieus that influence human conduct. It is imperative to observe business etiquette by duly recognizing and valuing cultural subtleties during interactions. Cultural intelligence in the realm of business encompasses a multitude of aspects,

including negotiation strategies and communication models.

3. **CQ Strategy:** Adaptability: Cultural intelligence is demonstrated through the capacity to modify communication and conduct based on the nuances of various cultural contexts. This flexibility is crucial for establishing rapport and preventing misunderstandings. Professionals with cultural intelligence demonstrate exceptional proficiency in establishing and nurturing relationships that transcend cultural boundaries. They exhibit proficient interpersonal abilities that facilitate cooperation and overcome differences.

4. **CQ Action:** Nonverbal Competence: Nonverbal signals frequently bear considerable weight in international business. Culturally intelligent people are sensitive to these signals and ensure that their nonverbal exchanges conform to the norms and expectations of the culture. Cross-Cultural Problem Solving: A proficient level of cross-cultural intelligence enables professionals to confront challenges from a standpoint well-informed by cultural factors. It requires finding solutions that resonate with various stakeholders and resolving conflicts.

Cultural intelligence's significance in international business:

- **Establishing Trust and Relationships:** Cultural intelligence is the cornerstone of establishing trust. The trust serves as a currency in international business before transactions. Respecting and appreciating the cultural milieu cultivates enduring and robust interpersonal connections.

- **Mitigating Misunderstandings:** Implementing cultural intelligence serves as a protective measure against misinterpretations that could disrupt business initiatives.

This capability enables professionals to identify prospective challenges and adeptly manage expectations proactively.

- **Strengthening Communication:** The foundation of prosperous international business is efficient communication. Cultural intelligence regulates the reception of messages to prevent misinterpretations that could result in misaligned goals by ensuring that they are not only comprehended but also received in the intended spirit.

- **Gaining a Competitive Advantage:** Possessing a team with a high cultural intelligence confers a competitive advantage in a globalized market. Business enterprises are empowered to adjust to evolving global environments and exploit nascent prospects promptly.

- **Promoting Innovation:** Innovation is fueled by diverse perspectives. Promoting an environment that values ideas from diverse cultural contexts is the essence of cultural intelligence. This variety of ideas has the potential to generate novel products and solutions.

Summary

The seventh chapter examines the opportunities and challenges of cross-cultural and international networking. The chapter commences by providing an analysis of cultural intelligence as it pertains to networking, elucidating the aptitudes required to thrive in international relationships. This segment underscores the significance of comprehending diverse cultural conventions, modes of communication, and protocols in the business world. It provides:

- Pragmatic guidance on cultivating cultural sensitivity.
- Acquiring knowledge of regional customs.
- Circumventing cultural blunders.

By developing cultural intelligence, individuals can foster more robust connections with those from various cultural contexts.

The chapter then examines the construction of international networks, emphasizing sophisticated cross-border tactics for establishing global linkages. This segment delves into strategies for augmenting one's network internationally, utilizing conventional and digital methods. This study explores strategies for establishing connections with individuals worldwide, attending international professional events, and using online platforms to fulfill this objective. Additionally, the segment discusses the complexities associated with global networking, including disparities in time zones and language barriers, while offering remedies to surmount these impediments.

The chapter concludes with a discussion of how to establish and maintain successful global partnerships in the face of various business environments. Prioritizing trust, mutual comprehension, and respect, it describes the procedures necessary to develop fruitful partnerships with international counterparts. This segment provides recommendations regarding cross-cultural negotiations, cross-border project management, and sustaining enduring partnerships with global stakeholders. The reader acquires the knowledge and skills necessary to navigate the intricacies of international business relationships and construct a transnational network. By implementing these tactics, they can strategically position themselves for success in an ever more interconnected global landscape.

"Networking is not about just connecting people. It's about connecting people with people, people with ideas, and people with opportunities." – Michele Jennae

Chapter 8: Taking Advantage of International Opportunities

In this chapter we explore strategies for expanding your networking reach globally:

- **Master International Seminar Etiquette**: Develop the skills to effectively communicate and network in international settings. Understand cultural nuances, practice active listening, and prepare thoughtful questions to engage with a diverse range of professionals and gain new insights.
- **Build Strategic Global Alliances**: Learn to identify and approach key global players and potential partners. Establishing influential alliances with international counterparts can open doors to new opportunities, collaborations, and innovative concepts across different markets.
- **Expand Your Transcontinental Network**: Utilize online platforms, professional associations, and international events to connect with professionals from various regions. Foster these connections through consistent communication, mutual support, and knowledge exchange to create a robust, worldwide professional network.
- **Implement Advanced International Job Search Techniques**: Acquire sophisticated strategies for searching and applying for jobs on a global scale. Tailor your resume and application to different cultural expectations, leverage international job boards, and utilize your global network to uncover hidden opportunities and gain a competitive edge in your career.

Organizations must have a global perspective to succeed in today's linked universe. One approach to accomplishing this goal is via the phenomenon known as international networking, which refers to establishing and sustaining connections with individuals and organizations hailing from various nations and cultural backgrounds. Accessing new markets, ideas, and resources is only one of the many advantages that may be gained via global networking. Additionally, it provides opportunities for personal and professional development, as well as opportunities for cooperation and knowledge of other cultures. From a commercial point of view, global networking has the potential to assist in the enhancement of sales, the enhancement of competitiveness, and the promotion of innovation.

The following is a list of some of the advantages of global networking:

1. Access to new markets: When you grow your network worldwide, you create opportunities for yourself to reach new clients and markets. This may bring a rise in sales and income and provide prospects for expansion.

If you are a software firm with headquarters in the United States, for instance, you can consider expanding your network to include businesses located in Europe and Asia. This may assist you in entering new markets and connecting with clients who might be interested in the items or services that you provide.

2. Idea generation: Ideas may be generated via global networking, which can also create chances for innovation and the production of new ideas. Interacting with individuals from a variety of cultures and backgrounds can expose one to new ways of thinking and approaches to problem-solving.

For example, if you are working on a new project, you can consider reaching out to individuals in your network who have knowledge in a variety of fields. This may allow you to come up with fresh concepts and methodological methods that you would not have thought of otherwise.

3. Understanding between different cultures: Global networking may be an effective tool for fostering communication and understanding. Cultural variations may affect business practices and relationships, making this a crucial component of doing business in today's global economy.

For instance, if you are working with a group of people from a foreign nation, you may need to be aware of the cultural variations in terms of communication techniques, work ethics, and business procedures. Cultivating connections with people from other cultures can help you gain a deeper comprehension of these distinctions and acquire the skills necessary to collaborate successfully with individuals from various backgrounds.

Thriving in Global Conferences and Seminars

Startups aiming to expand abroad might benefit from international conferences. Conferences are great for networking and showcasing companies and services. However, going for the first time might be intimidating.

Set objectives to maximize your international conference.

Set objectives before attending an international conference. Start by setting specific goals, such as meeting possible customers or investors, learning about industry trends, or forming business relationships. After setting objectives, create a strategy to achieve them. This may entail researching essential connections, attending sessions, honing your pitch to create a good impression, or making a list of networking questions. Setting objectives and making a strategy can help you maximize your conference time and accomplish your goals.

Plan your schedule

Managing your schedule at an international conference takes time and effort. Choosing one might take a lot of work for so many seminars and activities. Review the conference schedule in advance and choose sessions that align with your objectives to maximize your time. Consider each session's presenters, themes, and results, and prioritize those that meet your goals. It's also crucial to allocate time for unexpected opportunities or encounters. You'll learn and connect during the conference by arranging your schedule and being open to new experiences.

Network, network, network

Networking is crucial in international conferences. Meet new individuals and grow your professional network. Be confident, introduce yourself to industry peers, exchange business cards, and follow up after the convention. You never know when a new relationship may lead to business or partnership. To impress, prepare a brief pitch that showcases your unique value offer. Networking is about creating connections and becoming an industry expert, not merely selling your company.

Be open-minded

Attending an international conference lets you learn from industry professionals and peers. It's vital to prioritize sessions related to your objectives, be open-minded, and investigate non-business themes. New and inventive ideas may provide you with a competitive advantage. Attending many courses will teach you more about your sector and prepare you for problems. Engagement with other ideas and backgrounds is part of being open-minded. This will help you meet new people and create connections. Accepting new ideas and viewpoints may maximize your international conference experience and obtain an industrial edge.

Follow-up

Building relationships after the conference requires following up with individuals you meet. Personalize your message to indicate you cherish your time together. Referring to conference specifics or subjects may personalize and remember the message. If you are committed to supplying information, do so promptly. You may also arrange a follow-up meeting or call to continue the discussion. Keep track of your contacts and interactions in a spreadsheet or CRM. This might help you arrange and follow up on possibilities quickly. You show professionalism and a genuine interest in creating relationships by following up.

Strategic International Collaborations: Forging Partnerships with Impact

Within the dynamic realm of technology, the path to progress and ingenuity frequently extends beyond possessing an original concept or an exceptional product. Establishing connections, partnerships, and collaborations is equally significant.

Leveraging the Potential of Strategic Alliances

Success and survival in the dynamic and competitive technology and clean technology sectors frequently hinge on the capacity to establish licensing and distribution, OEM (Original Equipment Manufacturer), and OEM (Original Equipment Manufacturer) relationships. These strategic alliances serve as more than mere business transactions; they demonstrate the potential of combined capabilities by providing access to unexplored markets, technologies, and areas of expertise.

Using strategic alliances, especially those about technology (including consumer, commercial, hardware, software, IoT, mobile, and infrastructure sectors), innovative solutions are co-developed, and new markets are penetrated. By combining their resources and specialized knowledge, businesses can investigate unexplored markets, thereby increasing their comprehension of consumer demands and market penetration. These collaborative efforts frequently result in the development of groundbreaking products that both parties can create, exemplifying the profound impact of partnership.

Collaboration to Open Market Doors

Strategic partnerships enable businesses to penetrate new markets and demographics by capitalizing on their combined strengths to benefit both parties. By adopting this strategy, one can enhance their market penetration and stimulate the creation of innovative resolutions to intricate market obstacles. What was the result? An effortless expansion into previously inaccessible markets and regions due to the constraints imposed by single-entity initiatives.

Cultivating Innovation

Collaboration accelerates innovation, which leverages a wide range of resources and expertise. Allows partners to engage in ambitious projects while sharing risks and rewards, facilitates accelerated development cycles, and expedites introduction of state-of-the-art products to the market. This collaborative innovation expedites the development cycle and increases the attractiveness and competitiveness of the final products.

Strategic Determinations and Possible Obstacles

Effectively maneuvering through strategic partnerships necessitates a mutual interest and an extensive comprehension of the complexities and prospects inherent in these alliances. The subsequent critical variables necessitate consideration:

- **Vision and Objectives:** Harmonizing objectives and vision is a fundamental element of any prosperous partnership. A lack of synchrony can foster discord, diminishing the partnership's potential value.

- **Intellectual Property (IP) Protection:** Safeguarding intellectual property (IP) entails adeptly managing the intricacies associated with IP rights. Maintaining distinct boundaries between ownership and utilization rights is critical to mitigate conflicts and protect innovations.

- **Cultural Compatibility:** Cultural compatibility between corporations and the success of partnerships is of the utmost importance. The harmonious integration of work ethics, communication styles, and decision-making processes can enhance collaboration efficacy.

- **Considerations for Scalability and Flexibility:** Choose business partners who can expand with your organization. Adjusting to changing circumstances and potential advantages is vital in maintaining the partnership's pertinence.

- **Developing Exit Methods:** Several partnerships need to endure the test of time. Implementing fair and just exit strategies from the beginning can help reduce potential negative consequences and maintain professional connections.

International Job Hunting: Advanced Networking for Global Opportunities

As the globe becomes more interconnected, the notion of professional advancement has surpassed national boundaries. Modern aspirations transcend the confines of the nation-state.

Exploring International Job Markets

1. Understanding the Global Landscape

With the constant evolution of international job markets, a strong understanding of worldwide trends is crucial to achieving success. To commence this endeavor, we will offer insightful insights into sectors experiencing extraordinary growth in various nations. This understanding functions as a fundamental basis, enabling one to identify and predict the industries positioned for significant expansion. Equipped with this understanding, your capacity to align your distinct abilities and ambitions with the ever-changing and evolving demands of the global labor market transforms into a strategic edge. By aligning your interests and goals, you improve your ability to obtain significant employment and establish yourself as an active participant in influencing the global economy. In light of the dynamic nature of international opportunities, it is crucial to comprehend these developments to navigate a trajectory that harmonizes one's personal and professional ambitions with the constantly shifting requirements of the worldwide employment sector.

2. Conducting Opportunity Research

Undertaking an international professional trajectory is a significant undertaking that requires rigorous research adherence. Due to the complexities of international labor markets, a strategic plan is needed; this initiation entails an examination of opportunities that transcend national boundaries. A comprehensive roadmap awaits you, whether engaging with the extensive realm of online job listings, seeking the counsel of recruitment agencies, or immersing yourself in the opulent fabric of international career fairs. During this endeavor, we serve as reliable mentors, providing you with the necessary resources to recognize and capitalize on opportunities that perfectly align with your career goals. Every engagement with recruitment agencies brings you one step closer to realizing your aspirations, every online job board serves as a potential gateway to a global career, and every attendance at international career fairs presents an opportunity to establish connections that may profoundly influence your professional path. We guarantee that your research is well-informed, focused, and purpose-driven in every undertaking. International success is achieved through the application of knowledge gained from exhaustive research. By adhering to our strategic path, you will discover opportunities that unlock doors to rewarding positions, align your abilities with the demands of the global community, and ultimately craft a prosperous international career that mirrors your aspirations and enthusiasm.

3. Legal and Cultural Nuances

Adapting to a foreign work environment entails more than a simple change in circumstances; it constitutes an intricate and multifaceted experience. Cultural awareness and compliance with legal structures cannot be emphasized enough in this context. Acquiring substantial insights into cultural nuances assumes critical importance in this particular context, given their inherent influence on job searches and the definition of workplace dynamics. Gaining an awareness of these intricacies enables one to navigate professional environments adeptly, promoting efficient exchanges of ideas and amicable engagements.

Summary

You just completed Chapter 8 of the book, networking expert! This chapter discusses the potential of international opportunities and provides recommendations for cross-border networking. The chapter commences with a segment devoted to flourishing in international conferences and seminars, underscoring the significance of such gatherings in broadening one's global network. It offers guidance on optimizing these opportunities, including comprehensive preparation, active participation of presenters and attendees, and post-event follow-up. Additionally, this segment explores cultural subtleties that may impact engagements during international conferences, urging readers to exercise cultural sensitivity and flexibility.

The subsequent chapter explores strategic international collaborations, emphasizing establishing influential partnerships. This segment elucidates the advantages of collaborating with global counterparts and delineates tactics for establishing fruitful alliances across national boundaries. It includes identifying prospective companions, establishing effective communication, and establishing shared objectives. This segment demonstrates effective international collaborations and examines strategies for achieving outcomes advantageous to all parties involved. By appreciating the intricacies of cross-cultural collaborations, individuals can establish robust and enduring associations with stakeholders on an international scale.

The concluding segment of the chapter guides readers on how to utilize sophisticated networking techniques when seeking employment opportunities abroad. This segment addresses the complexities of cross-border job searching, including researching international job markets and customizing resumes to suit diverse cultural contexts. It guides effectively utilizing online networking platforms, establishing connections with recruiters worldwide, and participating in global career fairs. Mastering these techniques can give readers more opportunities and enhance their career prospects. By adopting an appropriate strategy, they can effectively establish connections and prosper in the international labor market.

"Everyone should build their network before they need it." – Dave Delaney

Chapter 9: Crisis Management and Networking Resilience

Networking isn't always positive and can come with its own set of challenges. Common saying goes "The commonly quoted phrase "any publicity is good publicity." Is just plain wrong.

This chapter is about navigating networking through challenging times and bouncing back stronger. Over the next few pages, we will:

- Learn to maintain relationships and overcome obstacles during crises with strategic focus.
- Analyze strategies for rebuilding your network after reputational losses.
- Restore trust and relationships effectively.
- Understand the principles of networking resilience.
- Surmount challenges with renewed strength and an expanded professional network.

Professionals need networking resilience to overcome difficult situations, bounce back from setbacks, and keep moving forward. Crisis management requires a proactive and purposeful approach to networking to enable individuals to utilize their resources and connections effectively during turbulent times. This chapter discusses the significance of crisis management, networking resilience, and techniques for building resilience in the face of difficulty.

Professionals must be adept at crisis management in today's fast-paced, unpredictable corporate world. Crises may affect people's jobs and means of subsistence in various ways, such as economic downturns, natural catastrophes, political unrest, and worldwide pandemics. Effective crisis management entails predicting, planning for, and reacting to crises in a timely and planned way to minimize harm and maximize recovery.

The capacity to change course, prosper in the face of difficulty, and use successful networking techniques is known as networking resilience. In times of crisis, people must make the most of their professional networks, assets, and abilities to overcome obstacles and grasp chances. Using networking resilience, professionals may sustain their career momentum, develop resilience, and emerge stronger from crisis circumstances.

Keeping solid connections with your professional network is essential for crisis management and networking resilience. In times of need, your network may provide invaluable assistance, counsel, and opportunities to help you overcome difficulties and roadblocks. By cultivating relationships with mentors, industry contacts, and colleagues, professionals may have access to many resources, information, and experience. These connections are very beneficial in trying times.

Another crucial component of crisis management and networking resilience is effective communication. Professionals should be open and proactive when discussing their difficulties and strategies for overcoming them with their network. When there is a crisis, professionals may mobilize peer support by being aware and involved in their network, which helps to establish credibility.

Flexibility and adaptability are essential traits for building networking resilience amid catastrophes. Professionals must exhibit flexibility and openness toward novel prospects, even if they deviate from their customary career trajectory or zone of comfort. By being adaptable and welcoming of ambiguity, professionals better position themselves to take advantage of new possibilities and overcome obstacles.

Creating an inclusive and varied network is essential for networking resilience in emergencies. A varied network may provide workers access to many viewpoints, ideas, and tools that can aid in navigating challenging and quickly evolving circumstances. By interacting with people from various backgrounds, sectors, and places, professionals may gain new insights and creative solutions to problems and grasp opportunities.

In today's turbulent business environment, crisis management and networking resilience are essential skills for professionals seeking to overcome hurdles and seize opportunities. Professionals who maintain excellent relationships, effective communication, and flexibility, adaptability, and self-care routines may create resilience and thrive in adversity. Professionals adopting the right mindset and coping methods may position themselves for long-term career success and emerge stronger from crises.

Networking during Crisis: Navigating Adversities with Skill

Effective networking becomes useful during difficult circumstances and a professional's lifesaver while facing uncertainty and misfortune. The capacity to use networks becomes essential for people to weather the storm and come out stronger, regardless of whether they are dealing with economic downturns, natural catastrophes, worldwide pandemics, or other unanticipated difficulties. This chapter examines the value of networking in times of crisis and techniques for skillfully overcoming obstacles.

Networking during a crisis is about building real connections and mutually supportive relationships that provide priceless assistance and opportunity during trying times. It is about more than passing business cards or engaging in conversation. Professionals need to understand that crises may impact everyone and that people can overcome hardship more successfully if they band together and support one another.

Keeping the lines of communication open with your network is essential during a crisis. Professionals must contact their contacts regularly to assist, check-in, and share pertinent resources and information. Encouraging honest and open communication within their networks can foster trust and camaraderie. This promotes a supportive environment that helps everyone get through the crisis together.

Another essential component of networking in a crisis is adaptability. Professionals must be flexible enough to modify their networking tactics and methods in response to the evolving conditions of the crises. This might include switching from in-person to virtual networking events, investigating novel approaches to maintaining connections with contacts, and adopting creative methods to remain involved and connected despite physical distance or other constraints.

During times of crisis, people may experience elevated levels of stress, worry, and uncertainty. In these circumstances, taking care of oneself is crucial. Professionals need to put their own mental health and well-being first. They should turn to colleagues, their network, and mental health specialists for help when necessary. People who prioritize their well-being are better equipped to handle the difficulties posed by the crisis and continue to be productive in their networking and other endeavors.

For people to effectively navigate through crisis circumstances, strategic networking is necessary. Building connections with essential stakeholders, business titans, and decision-makers who can provide insightful opinions, helpful resources, and support during trying times should be the main emphasis of professionals' networking activities. People may access possibilities, remain current on industry advances, and position themselves for success by discovering and cultivating strategic contacts once the crisis passes.

One of the main characteristics of successful crisis networking is resilience. When faced with difficulties, professionals must maintain their resilience and see them as opportunities for personal development and education. By keeping an optimistic outlook, being flexible, and enduring setbacks, people may go beyond challenges and become stronger on the other side of a crisis.

People should remember that, in times of crisis, networking is about giving back to one's network as much as receiving from it. Fostering goodwill, fostering connections, and providing support, direction, and help to others in their network may improve their professional community's resilience.

Rebuilding After Reputational Challenges: Advanced Networking Damage Control

Advanced networking damage management becomes crucial for those trying to restore their professional position and win back confidence in their network and sector in the aftermath of reputational issues. Rebuilding one's image and making good progress may be greatly aided by the capacity to skillfully handle reputational obstacles via strategic networking, regardless of whether one is experiencing public scrutiny, bad press, or personal failures.

The first stage in advanced networking damage management is owning up to any errors or blunders that may have contributed to the reputational difficulty and admitting that it exists. People must be accountable and transparent in their behavior, demonstrating a sincere desire to resolve the problems and, if necessary, make reparations. Individuals may regain credibility and confidence in their network by owning up to their mistakes from the past and showing a commitment to learn and improve.

After facing assaults on one's reputation, rebuilding requires strategic networking. Building connections with essential stakeholders, decision-makers, and influencers who may assist them in navigating the crises' aftermath requires individuals to be focused and purposeful in their networking activities. A person's attempts to restore their reputation may benefit significantly from the opportunities, support, and direction of establishing and maintaining strategic relationships.

When someone's reputation is threatened, peers and coworkers could be more skeptical of them and scrutinize them more closely. It becomes crucial to keep lines of communication open and be transparent with their network in these circumstances. People need to be proactive in responding to any queries or worries that could come up, giving honest and transparent accounts of the actions they are doing to resolve the reputational issue and constructively make progress.

People rebuilding their reputations after facing setbacks must also concentrate on showcasing their worth and knowledge in their field. To make a significant contribution to their area and establish themselves as thought leaders and subject matter experts, professionals should make the most of their abilities, expertise, and experience. People may repair their reputations and win back the respect and confidence of their peers by exhibiting their competence and contributing significantly to their sector.

People should also prioritize personal growth and self-improvement as part of their attempts to rebuild their reputations. Improving their knowledge and abilities may include looking for opportunities for professional development, such as more training, schooling, or certifications. People may show dedication to ongoing development and progress by investing in their professional and personal growth. This can help them regain trust and reputation in their network.

Advanced networking damage control tactics prioritizing responsibility, transparency, strategic relationship-building, and personal growth are necessary to recover following reputational issues. People may recover from reputational losses by reestablishing credibility and trust within their network, taking responsibility for their previous errors, and showing a desire for continuous development. People may overcome reputational issues and emerge stronger, more resilient, and more recognized within their sector by taking a proactive and deliberate approach to networking.

Networking Resilience: Emerging Stronger from Challenges

The capacity to overcome obstacles and become stronger professionally is known as networking resilience. Professionals often face challenges in today's fast-paced, cutthroat corporate world, which may try their perseverance and affect their path in the industry. On the other hand, those who have great networking resilience have the abilities, perspective, and network of allies needed to overcome obstacles and come out stronger on the other side.

Networking resilience is the capacity to change course and adapt when faced with difficulties. Professionals who possess networking resilience understand that obstacles are an inevitable aspect of the job path and see them as chances for development and education. Rather than allowing setbacks to depress them, they use their network to look for assistance, direction, and fresh chances that will enable them to overcome hurdles and make progress.

People who are resilient in networking must also have an optimistic outlook when faced with challenges. Resilient professionals concentrate on finding answers and chances for growth rather than lamenting about previous mistakes or disappointments. With the help of their network, they believe they can overcome hurdles and accomplish their objectives, so they face problems with optimism and tenacity.

Resilience in networking also involves effective communication. Professionals must confidently and effectively communicate their requirements, objectives, and issues to their network. Through transparent and genuine communication, people may solicit advice and assistance from their peers, mentors, and coworkers. They can also use their network's combined knowledge and assets to surmount obstacles and achieve success.

Developing a robust support network is crucial for fostering networking resilience. Professionals must surround themselves with people who empower, encourage, and inspire them to keep going when things become hard. A network of supportive peers and mentors may be very helpful in times of need, whether via official mentoring programs, professional organizations, or casual networking groups.

Another aspect of network resilience is the capacity to welcome ambiguity and adjust to change. Professionals must be adaptable and fluid in their approach to networking and career development in today's quickly changing corporate environment. This might include developing new talents, investigating untapped markets or career prospects, or adjusting to shifting consumer preferences and technological advancements. Resilient professionals may position themselves for success by accepting change and being flexible.

Networking resilience is essential for professionals who want to overcome obstacles and succeed in their jobs. Individuals may develop resilience and surmount challenges with the aid of their network by keeping an optimistic outlook, communicating effectively, building a solid support system, and accepting change. By developing networking resilience, professionals may overcome hardship and become stronger, more resilient, and more successful in their jobs.

Summary

This chapter delves into crisis management and networking resilience, providing strategies for navigating adversity and emerging stronger.

Networking during a crisis requires specific competencies to manage adversity effectively. It involves sustaining relationships through difficult times by embracing flexibility, clear communication, and empathy. Adopting a proactive stance is crucial, as it includes offering strategies for assisting others and identifying opportunities to strengthen relationships amidst hardship. These methods ensure that connections remain robust and supportive, even in challenging circumstances.

Reconstructing reputational challenges necessitates sophisticated networking damage control methods after a crisis. Strategies for restoring and maintaining a positive image include admitting errors, exhibiting accountability, and demonstrating a commitment to positive change. Reestablishing contact with the network, restoring credibility, and rebuilding trust are vital steps in this process. Examples of successful damage control, along with essential procedures for managing public relations, guide readers in rebuilding relationships. Networking resilience focuses on strategies for emerging stronger from obstacles, viewing crises as learning opportunities and catalysts for growth. This includes cultivating adaptability, continuous learning, and developing robust support systems. A resilient mindset is crucial for confronting future challenges and sustaining meaningful relationships, ensuring that a network can thrive despite adversity, and achieving sustained success in both personal and professional pursuits.

By mastering the techniques outlined in this chapter, you can effectively navigate networking during crises, manage reputational challenges, and build a resilient network that supports long-term success.

"Everyone you'll ever meet knows something you don't." – Bill Nye

Chapter 10: Networking for Personal Growth and Impact

If you're still reading and enjoying these networking insights, my mission in writing this book is a success! This final chapter focuses on the powerful potential of networking for personal growth and social influence.

By the end of this chapter, you will:

- Learn to network purposefully, with a focus on social change and significant causes.
- Explore methods for continuous personal development and advancement by leveraging networking to enhance expertise and understanding.
- Discover ways to create a lasting impact on your community and beyond by turning your networking efforts into tangible contributions.

Networking is a path of meaningful connections and personal development beyond business cards and LinkedIn connections. A more nuanced approach involves using networking as a tool for personal evolution and significantly impacting the world, even though many people concentrate on networking for business development or job progress.

The Viewpoint of Personal Growth

When you approach networking from a place of personal development, you see every encounter as an opportunity to learn. Every discussion turns into a chance to learn something new, have your assumptions tested, and broaden your perspectives. It's about cultivating relationships supporting your development, not amassing contacts.

To use this strategy, think about taking these actions:

1. **Curiosity First:** Be curious in all you do, including networking events and interactions. Ask inquiries that demonstrate a sincere interest in the other person's background, objectives, and experiences. This kind of thinking facilitates richer, more interesting dialogue.

2. **Learning Reciprocity:** Share your expertise and experiences freely without anticipating anything in return. Giving freely encourages reciprocation, which starts a circle of growth for both parties.

3. **Think and Adjust:** Consider the lessons you took away from networking events and how they affected your viewpoint. Use these reflections to inform your subsequent actions and modify your strategy as you develop.

Making a Difference Through Networking

Networking has the potential to have a significant social and professional impact. Connecting with people who share your goals and values allows you to collaborate on initiatives, initiate projects, and support worthwhile causes.

The following is how to handle networking effectively:

1. **Determine Your Values:** Before networking for influence, decide which causes or problems are most important to you. This clarity will help you identify groups and people who share your values.

2. **Locate Your Group:** Look for organizations and communities that share your beliefs. Online forums, social impact groups, and professional associations may be useful for this.

Effective collaborations will probably result from these connections.

3. **Use Your Power of Influence:** As you establish a network of like-minded individuals, consider how your combined influence may affect change. Your network has the potential to be a positive influence in the world through business endeavors, community service, or activism.

Networking is a dynamic process that promotes personal growth and increases your impact rather than only being a transactional activity. You can discover new avenues for personal growth and good global impact by approaching them with an attitude of inquiry, reciprocity, and shared ideals.

Networking for Social Change: Influencing Causes You Believe In

Networking isn't just about advancing personal or professional goals; it's also a potent tool for driving social change and influencing causes individuals deeply believe in. In this situation, networking becomes a way to connect with groups, communities, and like-minded people to promote constructive social change. Using connections and relationships to amplify voices, organize resources, and bring about significant social justice and environmental protection change is known as networking for social change.

The power of collective action is at the core of networking to effect social change. Through forming connections with like-minded others, people may establish coalitions and alliances to promote topics they are passionate about. Through networking, different stakeholders more easily share ideas, knowledge, and resources, resulting in cooperation and synergy that can lead to more significant change than could be achieved by any one person working alone.

Building genuine connections based on mutual respect, trust, and principles is the foundation of networking for social change. Others must devote time and energy to cultivating relationships with others who are committed to improving their local communities and society. Through the cultivation of authentic connections, people may establish a network of support that offers inspiration, encouragement, and camaraderie in their advocacy endeavors.

Finding important decision-makers, influencers, and stakeholders who can affect change on the problems at hand is essential to effective networking for social change. Through deliberately cultivating relationships with people with power or influence, advocates may effectively disseminate their message, access resources, and use their combined influence to effect legislative changes, generate public awareness, or carry out grassroots projects.

Activating grassroots activists and community organizers is another aspect of networking for social change and establishing connections with well-known leaders and influencers. Advocates may access the grassroots knowledge, vigor, and fortitude that propel social movements and bring about long-term change from the bottom up by building relationships with people and groups operating at the grassroots level.

Compelling narrative and communication are essential components of social change networking. To engage and motivate people to take action, advocates must be able to communicate their message clearly and appealingly utilizing storytelling strategies. A compelling vision for change, personal stories, and emphasis on the human effect of social problems are ways that advocates may inspire people to support and join their cause.

Networking for social change is about using the combined strength of people and communities to promote constructive social change. Advocates may increase their influence and bring about significant change on the topics they are passionate about by interacting with critical stakeholders, building true connections, inspiring grassroots activists, using narrative and communication, and using digital platforms. Networking becomes a potent instrument for fostering a more fair, just, and sustainable society for all people rather than merely a way to achieve professional or personal objectives.

Personal Development through Networking: Strategies for Lifelong Growth

Networking is an effective lifetime learning and personal development technique, helping one's career progress and establishing professional relationships. Through smart networking opportunities, people may broaden their minds, acquire fresh insights, and develop the abilities and attributes necessary to succeed in their personal and professional endeavors. Under these circumstances, networking turns into a tool for ongoing education, introspection, and enrichment of the individual.

Seeking out other viewpoints and experiences is one method for networking to further one's personal growth. Interacting with people from different sectors, backgrounds, and cultures may cause people to question their preconceptions, develop new perspectives, and widen their worldviews. Talking with others with various backgrounds and viewpoints may inspire creativity, invention, and personal development, enhancing one's comprehension of the outside world and oneself.

Developing a growth mindset is another method for networking to further one's personal development. Through networking, people may take on new projects, ask for criticism, and learn from others. Even in the face of failures or hurdles, people may embrace possibilities for growth and development by approaching networking with curiosity, openness, and resilience. Networking evolves into a voyage of self-discovery and ongoing progress rather than just a way to accomplish predetermined objectives.

Networking allows people to recognize and capitalize on their abilities and capabilities. People may identify their special skills and attributes by interacting with people in their network and receiving comments, affirmation, and support. Through networking, people may show off their abilities, gain self-assurance, and go after opportunities that fit their interests and passions, all of which contribute to a person's fulfillment and happiness.

Networking makes peer support and mentoring possible, both priceless tools for personal growth. People may get direction, counsel, and encouragement to help them deal with difficulties, overcome roadblocks, and accomplish their objectives by interacting with mentors, coaches, and encouraging peers. Through networking, people may create lasting connections with peers and mentors who can act as reliable confidants and inspire them as they pursue their career and personal goals.

Personal development via networking is an ongoing process of expansion, self-awareness, and enrichment. By seeking out other viewpoints, developing a development mindset, recognizing one's strengths and abilities, learning new things, and using peer and mentor assistance, people may use networking to improve their personal and professional lives. Through networking, people may become the greatest versions of themselves and discover a transforming process beyond just achieving external objectives.

Building a Legacy: Transforming Networking into Lasting Contributions

Networking allows people to leave a lasting legacy through their contributions to others and society, transcending individual career successes and professional milestones. By using networking as a platform for meaningful relationships, cooperation, and impact, people may leave a beneficial legacy for future generations. This legacy can reach well beyond those in their immediate circle of influence.

Building genuine connections based on trust, respect, and similar values is one strategy for turning networking into long-lasting contributions. People may create alliances and partnerships that increase their influence and allow them to collectively take on bigger, more difficult tasks by connecting with others who share their vision and passion for changing the world. Building a legacy of cooperation and group action beyond individual accomplishments is made possible by these deep relationships.

Networking allows people to advise and assist others as they pursue their professional and personal development goals. By imparting their knowledge, wisdom, and experience to others, people may empower and inspire the next generation of leaders and changemakers and have a lasting influence that lasts long beyond their lifetimes. Networking-based mentoring connections can change people's lives and careers and leave a legacy of empowerment and mentorship lasting for years.

Networking allows people to use their resources, knowledge, and abilities to solve urgent social and environmental challenges. By establishing connections with groups and people who share their values, people may work together on projects, initiatives, and campaigns that tackle the underlying causes of social issues and develop long-lasting solutions. By contributing to worthwhile projects and activities, individuals may leave a legacy of invention and influence that enhances the lives of others and makes the world a better place than they found it.

Networking can turn individual successes into enduring contributions that influence history and leave a beneficial legacy for future generations. Through genuine relationship-building, mentorship, cause advocacy, and using one's resources and abilities to benefit society, people may utilize networking to leave a lasting influence far beyond their lives. In addition to being a tool for achieving career or personal success, networking also serves as a platform for changing people's lives and leaving a lasting legacy.

Summary

Great Job on reaching this milestone in your networking journey! In Chapter 10, we explore how networking can drive personal growth and foster social change, extending beyond mere professional objectives.

Networking for social change emphasizes using connections to advocate for meaningful causes. It highlights the importance of forming alliances with like-minded organizations and individuals. By guiding and connecting with advocacy groups, community leaders, and other agents of change, this approach empowers readers to leverage their networks for positive social and environmental transformations. This method underscores the significance of collaborative efforts in driving impactful change and creating a collective force for good.

On the other hand, networking for personal development focuses on networking as a continuous process of self-improvement and learning. It discusses strategies for building a diverse network to foster personal growth and broaden perspectives, offering tactics for finding mentors and embracing new challenges and opportunities. Readers are encouraged to remain open to new ideas and seek growth through their networks. The concept of legacy building is explored, highlighting how networking efforts can be converted into lasting contributions. This includes mentoring, community involvement, and supporting philanthropic initiatives, emphasizing considering the impact one wishes to have and how one network can help achieve it. Through these practices, readers can build a network that supports positive contributions at both individual and community levels.

By applying the principles in this chapter, you can ensure that your networking efforts not only yield personal benefits but also contribute to a sustainable and impactful global legacy.

"Networking is marketing. Marketing yourself, your uniqueness, what you stand for." – Christine Comaford -Lynch

Conclusion

Fantastic! You've embarked on a life-changing adventure with "Networking Like A Pro." At this point in the book, I want to thank you for following along. While I haven't dedicated my entire life to writing, I've devoted a significant portion of my time to sharing the knowledge I've gained over a 20-year career in PR and Business Development. My success is ultimately measured by how well I'm liked by people and businesses. If I am liked, I succeed in my role as a BD director and the face of the company.

Networking comes naturally to some, while others must learn it as a skill. I am fortunate to have an innate ability to network and connect. I hope you have found this book useful and that it adds value to both your professional and personal life. Please let me know via my social pages how you've applied your newfound knowledge. If you're interested in continuing your growth, join our online community, share your experiences, and check out our online courses.

"Networking Like A Pro" transcends traditional networking concepts, exploring a world where relationships are deep, teamwork is strategic, and lives are transformed. It involves more than business transactions; it's about mastering the art of building relationships and influence. This book offers a comprehensive guide to achieving the highest level of networking success through advanced tactics.

The journey from novice networker to master influencer involves creating alliances beyond self-interest, fostering relationships beyond superficial exchanges, and making lasting impressions. Strategic alliances and meaningful connections allow you to direct your networking activities and create waves of influence that reverberate over time and space.

As you delve into "Networking Like A Pro," you'll discover that networking is more than a skill; it's an art form requiring perseverance, patience, and a deep understanding of human dynamics. It involves navigating the nuances of human interactions, leveraging diverse perspectives, and using collective action to create real change. By understanding how to establish connections with advocacy groups, community leaders, and other agents of change, you can leverage your network to effectuate constructive social and environmental transformations.

The book also discusses strategies for building a diverse network to foster personal growth, expand your horizons, and find mentors. This segment delves into maintaining receptiveness to new ideas, embracing challenges, and actively pursuing growth opportunities through networking. By adopting this strategy, you can achieve your personal and professional goals, gain valuable insights, and develop new skills through your network.

Furthermore, "Networking Like A Pro" explores converting networking efforts into lasting contributions. This includes mentoring, community involvement, and supporting philanthropic initiatives. Consider the impact you wish to have and how your network can help you achieve it. Building a network that supports positive contributions at both individual and community levels ensures that your networking endeavors yield personal benefits and contribute to a sustainable global impact.

With the insights and knowledge gained from this book, you're prepared to embark on your journey to becoming a true networking expert. Use these advanced techniques wisely and diligently, understanding the power they have to improve not only your life but also the lives of those around you. With each strategic connection and productive collaboration, you'll reach your full potential as a significant industry leader and changemaker.

Remember, your achievements are in your hands. Your network is your most valuable resource, and the connections you make will shape your journey in ways you can't yet imagine. Never overlook a chance conversation that could lead to a great collaboration or lasting friendship; it could change your life's course.

Thank you for being part of this transformative journey. I wish you success in all your endeavors and hope you build many beautiful relationships along the way. May the connections you forge become the foundation upon which you build your career and achieve your dreams.

You are destined for greatness, so go out there and network like a pro.

To your continued success and beyond!

Emmelie Forsyth

Author and Founder of Network Like a Pro

If you enjoyed this book, please consider leaving an honest review online on the platform you purchased the book from OR by visiting the official company website. I'd love to hear from you and know how you have applied the skills and techniques learned from this book into your professional (and personal) life.

www.networklikeapro.com

"You NEVER know where a conversation will take you"

www.ingramcontent.com/pod-product-compliance
Lightning Source LLC
Chambersburg PA
CBHW070154230526
45471CB00002B/658